The Imperfect Crime

Pete Dove

Published by Trellis Publishing, 2021.

While every precaution has been taken in the preparation of this book, the publisher assumes no responsibility for errors or omissions, or for damages resulting from the use of the information contained herein.

THE IMPERFECT CRIME

First edition. July 4, 2021.

Copyright © 2021 Pete Dove.

ISBN: 979-8224070138

Written by Pete Dove.

THE IMPERFECT CRIME

PETE DOVE

Perfect Spot – Imperfect Crime

Considering it is man-made, Lake Seminole is something of a beauty spot. It is a meeting point of several kinds. The Flint River, Chattahoochee River and Apalachicola rivers all join forces there. Just as three rivers come together so do three States, with Alabama, Florida and Georgia each having borders which run along it.

Thousands of years ago, it was the home to the Seminole Native Americans although in those days just the rivers flowed through the region. Then, when the United States was still young, and Florida was yet to become a US territory, a fort was built there. Fort Scott was created in 1816, to protect the new country from Spanish invaders. Within five years, it was redundant. Florida became a part of the United States of America, and the fort was abandoned. Well over a century later, the land itself disappeared. The construction of the Jim Woodruff dam caused a backlog of water, and in 1958 the Army Corps of Engineers got to work. The stretch of paradise now known as Lake Seminole was born.

The waters themselves are alive with fish: black crappie, striped bass, chain pickerel, bluegill. The names are evocative of times past. Of lazy days sitting by the water's edge, of kids with homemade rods, shirtless and straw hatted. As well as fish, the lake is home to a wide variety of birdlife, especially songbirds, who adore the habitat of pines and hardwoods which border the waterway. Those kids, though, if they were wise, would not leap into the waters to enjoy a refreshing dip under the hot midday sun. Another type of animal has grown to find the lake an attractive home. A somewhat bigger variety that those mentioned before. A different classification as well. If Lake Seminole is home to birds and fish, and a natural attraction to human mammals large and small, it also spreads its watery wings over some large amphibians. Alligators. And they are best avoided.

Jerry Michael Williams had headed to the Lake for a spot of December duck hunting. Mike, as everybody called him, didn't come home again. The conclusion to draw was clear. The thirty-one-year-old had slipped, fallen into the chilly waters and drowned before falling prey to one or more of those large alligators that waited, barely visible, in the waters. The year 2000 was coming to a close, and the real estate appraiser would not be home for the New Year. It was December 16th, the sixth anniversary of his marriage to wife Denise, and the two had an eighteen-month-old daughter, Anslee, who would be forced to spend Christmas – and every day after – without her daddy.

But investigators could see a clear and likely answer to the conundrum of what had happened to Mike. His boat had been quickly found. It was moored – or more likely it had drifted – into a small cove towards the western edge of the lake. It had been little used that day. The tank remained full of gasoline although the engine was not running.

A forty-four-day search ensued. It revealed nothing. That did not surprise wildlife officials who had good knowledge of the darker side of the lake. Below the surface tree stumps abounded. After all, not that long ago the lake had been dry land covered with trees. Those stumps remained just below the surface in places. It was December, and the water was cold. Anybody falling in would not last long. Drowning was a serious risk, and once that happened, the alligators would gratefully consume a free meal. So, the conclusion was reached. Mike had set off in the boat, possibly still getting his hunting equipment sorted. The boat had hit a stump, the sudden movement throwing Mike overboard. Maybe he hit his head and lost consciousness. Maybe he just drowned. Meanwhile his boat, the engine cut out by the jolt of hitting the tree stump, drifted until stopped by the edge of the cove. As Mike's body floated to the surface, the alligators struck. Soon there was nothing left for the search teams to find.

One person, though, did not believe that this had happened. 'I knew from day one he was not in that lake,' said Mike's mother, Cheryl.

The Williams boys – Mike had an older brother, Nick – grew up in Bradfordville, which lays directly between Tallahassee, Florida and the state line. His dad was a Greyhound bus driver, and his mother worked as a day care provider. These were committed parents, who made every effort to put their children first. In order to save money, the boys grew up in a large trailer rather than a brick home – a double width version with plenty of room. It was the best compromise their parents could find. The money saved from building a more conventional home was used to educate the boys at the North Florida Christian High School.

Mike enjoyed a very successful school career. He was the student council president and played football for the team. He was an active member of the Key Club. This is an organization which helps young people to gain leadership skills through service. It was no surprise that such a community minded young man should go on to attend University. Mike majored in political science and urban planning at the Florida State University. But by then he had already got to know his future wife. In fact, Mike met Denise Merrell when he was just 15. It was about this time that he began to develop his interest in duck hunting.

Mike's academic career continued apace. By the time he was ready to graduate, he already had a good job lined up, working for the Ketcham Appraisal Group, where he was about to be employed as a property appraiser. Work became almost an obsession for Mike. The Ketcham CEO called him 'the hardest working man I ever saw' and such was his commitment that he would often head back to the office in the evenings. He married Denise in 1994 and continued his devotion to his career. Even after Anslee was born, he would frequently wait for mother and daughter to retire to bed, then head back to finish off some jobs, or take out some work he had brought home with him. Similarly, his duck hunting jaunts would sometimes end with a spell in the office before he arrived home.

If such a commitment to his job might sometimes put a strain on those around him, it certainly brought home the money. By the time of his disappearance, Mike was earning around $200,000 annually. Sufficient for the young family to have bought an up-market home in the suburbs.

None of this is to imply that Mike shirked his domestic duties. He adored Anslee in particular, and just as his parents had done for him and Nick, no doubt some of his excessive working hours were to ensure he provided for his own family. Sadly, in 2000, Mike's father died, and this seemed to be a salutary lesson about the frailty of life. Mike and Denise took out a life insurance policy for $1 million dollars, lest the worse should happen. It was sold to them by Brian Winchester. Brian and Denise had known each other since their childhood, and Brian had in turn become best friends with Mike.

With the sad exception of the death of his father, life for Mike, Denise and their little one seemed, on the face of it, very good. Mike was planning to take a sabbatical, if he could raise enough money to afford one. A cruise was booked to Hawaii for the Spring of 2021, and Mike was looking forward to a work trip to Jamaica. Best of all, they were looking to grow the family, and have a sibling for their daughter.

On the day of his disappearance Mike left the family home early, according to Denise. There was nothing unusual in this and given that they planned to go out later that day to celebrate their wedding anniversary, it made sense that he completed his day's plans as promptly as reasonable.

But by noon, there was no sign of Mike. He had been expected home earlier than that, and worried about their planned celebration in Apalachicola, Florida, Denise began ringing around to see if she could trace where her husband had gotten to. Several friends offered to head down to the lake to check if they could see Mike. Included amongst them was Brian Winchester, who had received a call from his own father telling him that Mike was missing. He and his father took their own boat out onto the lake to see if they could trace the missing man.

Soon, though, the light began fading, and so it was perhaps surprising that it was as darkness settled that they discovered Mike's boat. Nearby, his Ford Bronco was parked up. Of Mike, there was no sign.

Then, a few week's later, a discovery was made. Mike's jacket and waders, along with his hunting license, were discovered. This seemed to confirm that he had drowned. Given that no body had been seen floating to the surface, the conclusion that alligators had eaten his corpse grew in strength. In most quarters, at least. Cheryl never believed that her son had drowned, and then been consumed by local wildlife. If he had, then those particular alligators were possessed of the finest table manners. There was no sign of teeth marks or tears on the clothing at all.

It was during the following summer that Denise began to press John Crusoe, the Leon Circuit Judge, to make the call that her husband was dead. Although he was still considered a missing person by the police, they did not believe his remains would ever be found and the judge agreed.

Meanwhile, Cheryl would not let the case rest. She began petitioning local officials to reopen the case, and even began her own investigations. At one stage, she was writing daily to the Governor, and in the end her determination to get her son's case re-examined bore fruit. In 2010, police changed their classification of Mike's disappearance from 'missing person' to 'suspicious death', and a team of cold case investigators were given the task of looking again at such facts as they had.

But, by that time, a lot had happened. Including the remarriage of Denise. Her new husband was her childhood acquaintance and best friend of her irretrievably lost husband, Brian Winchester. Since Denise had pushed the judge to declare her husband as being officially dead, she had inherited the one-million-dollar insurance policy, along with two others he already held, bringing her windfall to $1.75 million.

It also emerged that Denise's second marriage did not result from a relationship formed after her first husband's death. In fact, she and Brian Winchester had been having an affair since 1997, more than three years prior to Mike's disappearance. Denise and Brian wed in 2005. Matters were beginning to look suspicious.

The cold case team made a number of discoveries. It just went to show how simple it is to tie things to an easy and convenient explanation if one exists. One of the first inconsistencies was the mismatch between the engine being off and the gas tank full. Unless Mike had fallen overboard before turning on the engine, then, according to the manufacturers, the engine would have kept running until the gas ran out.

Four options presented themselves. Firstly, the possibility that Mike had chuntered out to the middle of the lake, then turned his engine off before falling overboard. But the lake was not fast flowing, and it was hard to see what would make him fall out of his vessel if it was hardly moving. Further, there was no logical reason why he would head towards the middle of the lake, then decide to hang around there, drifting. Events were planned for the remainder of the day. He did not have hours to kill.

Secondly came the equally unlikely theory that Mike had boarded the boat in the cove, and immediately fell out, drowning in the process. The other two options were more feasible but offered sinister explanations. Could Mike have been attacked before he got onto the boat? Or was he attacked on the water and the assailant then turned off the boat's engine himself? In either case, the suggestion of foul play presented itself.

Other problems soon began to knock on the door. The thing was, Mike rarely went hunting alone. Why would he suddenly choose to do so on this particular day? Then there was the location of the boat. If, as now seemed most likely, Mike had not even made it out onto the water, then why had he picked a spot which was difficult to access? A concrete ramp was fairly near at hand. But his Bronco was close to where the boat was found. Which meant he had either dragged it back to the ramp to launch it in the water – a very strange thing to do if he was on his own – or forced it through mud to get to the water's edge. Something physically extremely difficult.

The plot quickly deepened. The alligator theory had seemed so neat and tidy. What else could explain the complete disappearance of a fully grown adult male's body? But the problem with theories is that they are hard to prove, but relatively easy to disprove. All that is needed is some research into what has happened. Something, it seemed, lacking in the initial police investigation, which was looking less and less competent by the moment.

Indeed, the discovery some years back of Mike's waders and jackets added to the idea that he had drowned, then been ripped from his clothing. The hunting gear was even discovered between a pile of alligator droppings and some torn weeds. Clearly, therefore, the droppings explained the presence of the beasts, and the damaged reeds evidenced that a struggle had taken place. Presumably, between an alligator and an inert corpse it was trying to rip from its clothing, without damaging the specialist attire.

As daft as that theory seemed when written down cold, further proof that it could not have happened came from a brief discussion with some experts. The issue was that Mike disappeared in the depths of winter, and North Florida alligators do not feed during these colder months. Even if they did, explained the people who knew what they were talking about, they would not consume an adult human male whole. Traces would be left.

But although it suddenly seemed likely that a crime had taken place, police had no clue as to who might be behind it. Cheryl, though, did. She suspected that her former daughter in law and her new husband might have played a part in the death of her son. 'They're the only two people that profited from Mike's disappearance,' she claimed later.

Cheryl also put to bed any theories that Mike could have staged his own disappearance. She explained that he was a good and popular man, with many friends. Also, that he loved his daughter 'more than life itself.' He would not, could not, abandon her. Although, it seemed, Cheryl was prevented from seeing her granddaughter. 'She was the only thing I had left of Michael,' she said, putting her trauma into context.

But whilst investigators were making little further headway as they delved into the case of Mike's disappearance, elsewhere matters were coming to a head. Denise and Brian were discovering that they were not a match made in heaven. In fact, things were turning so bad that Denise wanted a divorce. According to some reports, it was his addiction to sex that had turned her away. Brian, though, wanted them to stay together. And it transpired that he was prepared to go to extreme lengths to get his way.

It was August 5th, 2016, and in the early hours of the morning when Denise opened the trunk of her SUV. She got a nasty shock. Inside lay the husband from whom she had recently separated. And he held a gun. Brian was furious. He demanded that Denise get back together with him, that she abandoned any ideas of a divorce. Denise feared for her life. And for that of Anslee's. Although Brian claimed that the gun was to be used to shoot himself, not her. 'Is today the day the two of us die?' she reported asking her estranged husband, to which he replied, 'just me.'

Still, Denise was terrified. She managed to calm Brian down, insisting that she in fact did not want a divorce, had changed her mind and would return to living with him. He was pacified enough for her to drive him back to his own truck, and she claimed that he then disinfected the back of her own SUV. They drove away in their separate vehicles, before she found him once again next to her at a stop light, where he apologized for his actions and drove off.

Denise, though, was not finished with the matter. She headed straight to the police and reported that she had been subject to a domestic kidnapping. The police moved quickly, and Brian was soon arrested. He was charged with a number of offences. These included domestic assault and armed burglary as well as kidnapping. Denise also requested protection from her estranged husband, whom she feared could assault her again, or her daughter. The court was sympathetic, and Brian was held without bond. Meanwhile, he was concerned, apparently, about what Denise might tell the police about something strange. The matter involved, according to testimony, 'This guy who died 10 or 12 or 15 years ago.'

Let us consider the comment for a while. It is an odd statement. Brian is an intelligent man, working in insurance. A death is a serious matter and were he to be involved in whatever had taken place he would surely have held a clearer picture of when the incident had occurred. Or, perhaps, this was an attempt to create a smokescreen. For Cheryl Williams, the arrest gave hope that a resolution might be found to explain Mike's death. It was clear that her suspicions still lay towards Denise. 'I'm praying he (Brian Winchester) doesn't commit suicide,' she said. 'I'm praying he'll tell us what actually happened.'

A small part of her still believed that Mike might still be alive, although it was widely accepted at this time that he must be dead. 2017 saw dramatic progress. But not in a cheering way. Brian Winchester was sentenced to twenty years for the kidnapping. In the immediate aftermath of this, the announcement was made that Mike's body had been discovered. He had been murdered. DNA checks to Cheryl proved beyond any shadow of a doubt that the remains discovered were those of Mike.

With Brian already in prison, the authorities turned their attention to Denise Williams. But they knew that to capture her, they would need the help of her former husband. It seems as though he was willing to provide it. It was May 8th, 2018. The day of Anslee's nineteenth birthday. She had spent the overwhelming majority of these without her dad and was about to lose her mom as well. With little regard to the sensibilities of Anslee, Denise was arrested on that day. Having waited for so long, it seems odd that the police could not hang on for another twenty-four hours. Could not save a daughter a little suffering. Whilst she may have been a murderer, Denise was clearly no threat to anybody else. But they chose not to wait, and Denise was indicted on the charges of first-degree murder, of conspiracy to commit that murder and as an accessory after the fact. Further charges relating to insurance fraud would follow on before too long could pass.

It certainly seemed as though any vestiges of feelings for each other that once existed between Denise Williams and Brian Winchester were well scattered to the winds. An unedifying series of claims and counter claims followed, each attempting to place the blame for Mike's death firmly on the shoulders of the other. Denise totally denied the charges against her. She insisted that it was her then husband to be who was completely responsible for the homicide. Winchester's defense was a tad more subtle; but only very, very slightly so. Yes, it was he who had killed Mike, but on the instructions of the women with whom he was already infatuated.

Friendship with her had turned to passion at a music concert, and between that day in 1997 and their marriage eight years later they had, he admitted, conducted an intense but secret affair. He too was married at that time. But his wife, Kathy, knew nothing of the goings on. In fact, as far as she was aware up until Mike's disappearance, they were two couples who happened to be best friends. Meanwhile, Brian and Denise were organizing their schedules in ways which allowed them to meet for lunch; even, sometimes, going off on vacation with each other. They would also meet illicitly at one another's houses when they knew that nobody was home.

And it was, he maintained, their love for each other that resulted in Denise's determination to kill not only her own spouse, but Brian's too. Love had, claimed the convicted kidnapper, sparked in high school, but that had been but a teenage romance. They had gone their separate ways yet still held feelings for each other, despite the paths their lives took. Only after that Sister Hazel concert did they think that they could not live without each other.

One day, according to Brian, he and Mike had gone together on a hunting trip. Mike had accidently fallen down a mud hole. The ground had collapsed beneath him, and the wet soil below had begun to drag him down. Both were convinced that had his friend not been there to save him, Mike could have died. The chances were that his body would never have been found, with the opening closing up after it had swallowed him.

When Brian and Denise were discussing the incident later, Denise began to suggest many ways in which they could get rid of Mike. When Brian suggested the easiest, that they each simply divorce their partners and bring their own relationship out in the open, he said that Denise shunned the sad but simple solution. Her family, she said, could never approve of divorce. Further, she could not bear sharing custody of Anslee with her then husband. Perhaps that explains the reason Cheryl was denied any access to her granddaughter for so long.

It was at this time, again according to Mike in his testimony at Denise's trial, that she urged him to do away with Kathy as well, although he refused to do so. Money, too, played its wicked role in their plans. Denise wanted Mike killed in a way that would ensure she got her hands on his insurance payouts.

Over time the plans centered on a boating accident. They began to formulate their final plans, until Denise got cold feet. They soon warmed up, claimed Brian, and she urged Mike to take the morning hunting on 16th December. Even though it was the day planned for their own anniversary celebrations, he was happy to do so, and met

Brian at their regular spot on Lake Seminole. Brian, though, had found an even better location for their spot of duck hunting, and directed Mike to it.

Now the truth about the boat came to light. They had taken it out onto the lake, and the plan was that Brian would push his former best friend and now love rival into the cold waters and leave him to drown. The plan failed. Mike found a tree stump and balanced himself on it while removing the heavy waders and jacket which were dragging him under. Another erroneous clue explained.

Seeing Mike about to rescue himself, Brian took the boat over to the stump and shot him in the face with a 12-gauge shotgun from point blank range. Who can imagine the confusion in Mike Williams' mind as he tries to process the actions of the man he believed to be his best friend?

Brian removed the body from the water, wrapped it in a heavy sheet, and drove to another area where he might find a mudhole. Discovering one, he weighted Mike's body and buried it. It would be nearly seventeen years before the remains would come to light.

The jury believed the account given by her former husband, and Denise Williams was sentenced to life imprisonment for her role in the homicide. A plea bargain ensured Brian would serve no longer than his current sentence.

There was one final twist, however. On appeal, Denise's conviction was overturned. The court decided that, since Denise did not aid or abet Brian in the homicide, and she did not hire him to carry out the crime, she could not be found guilty of first-degree murder. Instead, her sentence was altered to the thirty years she had already been awarded for her conspiracy to commit murder.

For Cheryl, it was a real kick in the teeth. 'I am sick,' she said when told of the news, 'It's like nobody is responsible for Mike's murder.'

Another victim of a cruel crime who has failed to find peace.

THE BRILLIANT SERIAL KILLER : THE TRUE STORY OF ISRAEL KEYES

MARK TOLBERT

Israel Keyes was an American serial killer who was active from approximately 2001 to his capture in 2012. He was known for his extreme attention to detail, his patience and discipline in selecting targets that lived far away from him. He was also meticulous in disposing of his victim's bodies as authorities have not uncovered any other evidence that Keyes did not provide.

Keyes killed several victims across the United States and was finally caught in 2012 after he uncharacteristically deviated from his modus operandi and hatched a plan to collect a ransom from his last victim's family.

Keyes was known to go to extreme lengths to hide his involvement in these murders, including driving across the country in rental cars, while using nothing but cash and removing the batteries from his cell phones in order to evade detection. This is uncharacteristic for a serial killer, since the vast majority of his contemporaries are known to have killed within their general geographic area.

While in federal custody in Anchorage, Alaska, Keyes would cooperate with investigators and admit to a host of crimes, including kidnapping, rape, and murder. Furthermore, Keyes admitted to committing a variety of burglaries and bank robberies to fund his killing sprees.

Early Life

Israel Keyes was born in Richmond, Utah in 1978. He was the second child to John Jeffrey Keyes and Heidi Hokansson. John, a maintenance man, and Heidi, a stay-at-home mom, raised their son in a Mormon environment and home-schooled both Israel and his eight siblings.

Soon after his birth, Israel's parents moved the family to Aladdin Road, a small area north of Colville, Washington. While his family officially followed the Mormon faith, they were known to attend a local Christian Identity church, an organization rumored follow a white supremacist version of Christianity. Some, however, dispute this label and liken the religion to having parallels with the Amish church.

The family also quickly became friends with the neighbors, the Kehoe family. Chevie Kehoe, the eldest of eight sons, would later become an infamous white supremacist and convicted murderer, after killing William Frederick Mueller, along with his wife and daughter, during a robbery to secure guns, ammunition, and money.

During his time in Aladdin Road, Israel became a very introverted child with little interaction with the other children in town. He built his own cabin at the age of sixteen and preferred the wilderness over people. He is known to have burglarized several houses during his time in Aladdin, however, and is believed to have killed family pets for entertainment.

"When I was fourteen there was some friends staying with us," Keyes recalled. "And there was this cat of ours that was always getting into the trash. I had a lot of guns and I would always carry a gun and I shot it in the stomach. And it ran around and around the tree...and then it like crashed into the tree. I actually kind of laughed a little I think but..and then I looked over at everybody else and the kid who was with me, he was throwing up. Like he was, really, I don't know (chuckles) traumatized I guess you would say."

"Like most serial killers," forensic psychiatrist Paula Orange said. "Keyes built himself up to killing people by killing small animals first."

Following his family's relocation to Smyrna, Maine to become involved in the maple syrup business in the late 1990s, Keyes was kicked out of his family home for rejecting his parents' faith. His parents told his siblings to stay away from him.

"Keyes didn't think too much of his family," Orange said. "He was raised in a cult-like atmosphere and rejected the family religion, becoming very outspoken out his lack of belief in God. He had a Satanic pentagram branded on his back as well as an upside-down cross on his chest."

The rejection made Keyes want to tour the country and burn down as many churches as he could. Instead, he turned to murder and rape.

His first violent crime was committed sometime between 1996 and 1998, when Keyes abducted a teenage girl and raped her. Despite his later penchant for murder, he allowed this victim to go free. The identity of the teenage girl remains unknown.

Military Career

In 1998, Israel Keyes decided to enlist in the United States Army while living in New Jersey. Keyes served as a specialist in the 1st Battalion, 5th Infantry. He was subsequently stationed at Ft. Lewis, near Tacoma, Washington, and at Ft. Hood, near Killeen, Texas. He would later receive training in the Sinai region of Egypt.

While serving in the U.S. Army, Keyes was awarded the Army Achievement Medal for "meritorious service while assigned as a gunner and assistant gunner from the 2nd of December 1998 to the 8th of July, 2001 in the Alpha Company 60mm mortar section." Although Keyes received a DUI in Washington state in May 2001, he left the U.S. Army with an honorable discharge later that year.

Keyes would settle in Alaska and get a job working in construction. Incredibly, he would draw rave reviews from his employer who had no idea of the double life his new carpenter with the long hair led.

"Keyes was described as someone who was very professional," Orange said. "He had a tremendous focus and would work on projects for hours on end with intensity and focus. He would not stop for lunch. He would just work straight on through."

Keyes was described in a favorable manner by just about everyone else who met him. Words like "friendly", "low-key", "reliable" were among the adjectives used to describe him.

"The secret life was power to Israel Keyes," Orange said. "He got off on the fact that everyone he encountered had no idea who or what he really was. To them, he was a friendly carpenter who was on the quiet side. Mellow. But inside he was a raging killer. That is what gave him power."

Crimes

Bill & Lorraine Currier

After receiving his honorable discharge from the United States Army, and sometime between April and May 2011, Israel Keyes constructed a homemade silencer for his Ruger .22 pistol. Once he decided to kill, Keyes booked a flight from Washington state to Indiana. After arriving in Indiana, Keyes rented a car and drove the remaining 1,000 miles to the East Coast of the United States, using cash-only for the duration of the trip to avoid leaving behind any evidence.

Keyes arrived in New York to test his homemade silencer, then traveled to Vermont to pick up a murder "toolkit" that he had buried two years before. Keyes soon found an abandoned farmhouse in Essex, Vermont, which he identified as the location he would take his next victim to before killing them. He initially targeted random drivers passing through the rural area, intending to shoot out a tire on their car and kidnap them after they crashed, but decided to focus on a married couple after dismissing his original plan as unpractical and dangerous.

He soon identified Bill and Lorraine Currier, living at 8 Colbert Street, as his next victims on July 8, 2011.

Bill and Lorraine were 49 and 55 years old respectively. They had just celebrated their 25th wedding anniversary. Bill worked at the local university as a lab assistant while Lorraine worked at a nearby medical center.

"They were good people," Orange said. "They had a lot of pride in the upkeep of their Vermont home, manicuring the lawn and planting flowers. They were good employees and well-liked by co-workers. They were the epitome of upstanding, normal good people."

Keyes had picked the Currier's because they had no dog, no kids and a garage that would let him into the house. He stalked them for days, knowing their comings and going.

As one investigator would note, "Keyes was a serial killer with a system."

In the middle of the night, Keyes disabled the Currier's phone line and entered their house in what has been described as a "blitz attack." He ambushed the couple while they were sleeping and quickly subdued them, tying the couple up and stealing Lorraine's .38 snub-nose revolver in the process.

Once the couple was secured, he proceeded to transport them to the abandoned farmhouse in Essex. During the course of the night, both Lorraine and Bill attempted to escape the house. Lorraine was successfully captured and re-restrained. However, Keyes shot Bill with his silenced .22 caliber Ruger pistol in a fit of rage during his escape attempt. After killing Bill, Keyes sexually assaulted Lorraine and strangled her to death in the basement.

Following the killings, Keyes buried Bill and Lorraine's bodies in the basement of the Essex farmhouse, intending to return to the house at a later date to set fire to the building and thereby destroy any evidence in the blaze. Once the bodies were buried, Keyes set out to commit a robbery spree using the Currier's car.

"Keyes was spotted driving the Currier's car," Orange said. "The eyewitness quickly relayed this information to the police and they were able to come up with a sketch of Keyes. They were reported missing by this time and the authorities knew that foul play was involved. Things became particularly worrisome as the man in Currier's car was driving alone and the couple was nowhere to be found."

The Currier's car soon suffered "serious mechanical issues" and Keyes decided not to go through with his crime spree.

Keyes quickly abandoned the Currier's non working car in an apartment parking lot at 203 Pearl Street and proceeded to the White

National Monument Forest to burn the couple's belongings and to bury his toolkit and handgun.

Unbeknownst to Keyes, the farmhouse containing the Currier's bodies was bulldozed from October 25-27, 2011. The bodies, along with the rest of the farmhouse, were unknowingly disposed of at the local landfill.

The resting place lived up to Keyes' motto, 'Out of sight, out of mind.'

Samantha Koenig

On February 1, 2012, Keyes began to search for another random victim. He identified 18-year old barista Samantha Koenig, living and working in Anchorage, Alaska, as his next victim.

Samantha worked at a walk-up kiosk on a relatively busy highway. It was snowing that night, however, and folks were driving by too fast to pay attention to the man who walked up to the counter in a ski mask. This would not be unusual in Anchorage as the weather was freezing. Samantha greeted Israel with a smile and he handed her his travel mug, asking for some coffee. She would turn back around he had a gun pointed at her.

"Turn out the lights," he commanded.

Samantha complied.

"Turn around," he said.

Samantha began to cry, complying with his command. He forced her to empty the register then tied up her wrists with cable wire. After finding out that Koenig had a boyfriend who was set to show up soon, Keyes laid in wait for the boyfriend, Duane Tortolani. However, he quickly abandoned his plan to capture a second victim and dragged Koenig to his truck before transporting her to his property.

The next day, February 2nd, Keyes broke into Koenig's house. While there, he also burglarized her boyfriend's truck, taking the couple's joint debit card with him. However, both Koenig's father and Duane Tortolani witnessed this burglary and notified the authorities.

Keyes quickly tested the debit card to make sure that it worked and, upon confirming that it worked, he returned to his home and quickly killed Koenig, leaving her body in a storage shed located on his property. He immediately traveled to New Orleans, where he set out on a week-long cruise. However, once he disembarked from the cruise Keyes became increasingly concerned over the media coverage and intense police investigation of Keonig's disappearance and set out on a crime spree.

On February 16, Keyes burglarized and burned down a home in Aledo, Texas. Shortly thereafter, Keyes robbed the National Bank of Texas, attempting to kidnap yet another woman he saw walking a dog. Luckily, this potential victim was able to escape.

Other Victims

Israel Keyes is suspected of killing or attempting to kill several other victims. Keyes' first admitted violent crime took place sometime between 1996 and 1998, when he abducted and raped a teenage girl in Washington state. Unlike his later crimes, Keyes did not kill this victim. He released her soon after the sexual assault.

"My entire goal was to stay under the radar," Keyes said. "For a lot of this stuff, there wasn't anything. All I can say is that unless I talk about it, you're never going to find any evidence."

His first suspected murder is of an unknown couple in Washington State in 2001. Keyes also claimed to have killed another unidentified victim in Leah Bay, Washington in July 2001.

He planned out his killings like most people plan out their vacations. He would travel far away from his location.

From 2005 to 2006, Keyes is suspected of killing two separate victims. He confessed to these murders while being held at the Anchorage Correctional Complex, saying that these murders were committed on two separate occasions. Furthermore, he claimed to have dumped one of the bodies in Crescent Lake, located in Oregon.

"There is a history of this stuff that goes back a long time," Keyes said. "It's not something I've ever talked to anyone about."

Keyes just didn't rape his female victims. He would rape his male victims as well. It was something he was ashamed of as well as his necrophilia.

Following a multi-year break from killing, Keyes admitted to killing Debra J. Feldman in Hackensack, New Jersey on April 8, 2009. He also claimed to have killed another victim the following day somewhere in New York state.

Keyes would bury his murder weapons across numerous fields across the entire United States. Because of his military training, he knew how to maintain the weapons and return to them after they had been out of use for years. He buried these weapons in canisters filled with cable ties, ropes and drain cleaner.

During these trips, Keyes would admit to frequenting prostitutes.

Lastly, following the murder of Samantha Koenig and during his travels throughout the Southwestern United States, Keyes claims to have killed an unknown victim in Texas. The identity and final location of this victim remain unknown.

In addition to the actual murders that he committed, Keyes admitted to attempting to kill several other individuals over the years. For example, Keyes admitted to attempting to shoot both a couple and male police officer in Anchorage, Alaska sometime between April and May 2011. He also admitted to attempting to kidnap and kill a woman he spotted walking her dog in Texas, just days before his capture by a combination of Texas and federal law enforcement.

Other Crimes

Keyes was known to commit burglaries and bank robberies in order to fund his killing sprees. In addition, he admitted to killing small animals from the time he was a young child. He is said to have killed an unknown number of family dogs and cats throughout his travels.

<u>April 10, 2009</u>

Keyes robbed the Community Bank in Tupper Lake, NY in order to fund his killing spree. After holding up the bank teller with a .40 caliber Smith & Wesson (and with a .22 caliber 10/22 Ruger pistol in reserve), Keyes made off with over $10,000 in cash. Although he was filmed on camera during the robbery, his use of sunglasses, uncharacteristic clothing, and a fake mustache prevented him from being identified.

Following the successful robbery, Keyes buried a box with his robbery supplies in the Woodside Natural Area in Essex, Utah. He returned home four days later with the $10,000 in his possession.

<u>February 16, 2012</u>

While Keyes was traversing across the Southwestern United States following the successful ransom for Samantha Koenig, he committed two additional crimes. First, Keyes committed arson by setting fire to and burning down a 3,500 square foot house in Aledo, Texas. Secondly, Keyes again committed a bank robbery by holding up a teller at the National Bank of Texas in Azle, Texas, making off with an undisclosed amount of cash.

In all, Keyes is suspected of committing some 20 to 30 home invasions and burglaries during his lifetime. Furthermore, he killed an unknown amount of animals from his childhood to capture and is believed to have committed several unidentified bank robberies during his adult years in order to fund his killing trips across the country.

Capture

After murdering Samantha Koenig and leaving Alaska, Keyes concocted a plan to demand a $30,000 ransom for Koenig's return (at the time, police were unaware that Koenig had been killed). Keyes texted his demands and instructions to Duane Tortolani, Koenig's boyfriend.

At the same time, Keyes dug up the body of Samantha Koenig, dismembered it, and disposed of the body in Matanuska Lake.

The case became a high-profile one and community members chipped in to meet the ransom demand.

Thirty-thousand dollars, courtesy of a concerned and frightened community, would be deposited into Samantha's account.

After receiving the ransom money, Keyes began withdrawing cash from the associated account using her stolen debit card. There would be withdrawals in Alaska. Then Arizona. Then New Mexico.

The authorities would always be fifteen minutes behind the suspect when he made these withdrawals.

Israel would wear a "Scream" mask while the withdrawals but his 2012 Ford Focus that he was drawing was identified. The FBI noted all of their counterparts to be on the lookout for Keyes in this vehicle. It is important to note that Keyes actually exchanged his rented 2012 Ford Focus for another car to avoid detection; however, the rental company provided him with another 2012 Ford Focus for his exchange. This would eventually help to lead to his capture.

Police were then able to track account withdrawals as he traveled throughout the Southwestern United States, having made withdrawals from Koenig's account using her debit card in New Mexico, Arizona, and Texas. Interestingly, authorities had a video of Koenig's abduction but refused to release the footage to the public, a controversial move that many outsiders saw as hampering his capture.

Having left his sister's wedding just days before (where he became embroiled in a contentious argument about his pronounced atheism), Keyes was spotted speeding along Highway 59 by a Texas Highway Patrolman on March 13, 2012.

"The patrolman that made the traffic stop had no idea that Keyes was a wanted serial killer," Orange said "Keyes did not have his gun handy at the time. If he had, there's no doubt in my mind that he would have started shooting."

Keyes was placed under arrest by the patrolman and the Texas Rangers as well as the FBI was brought in. Authorities found the following items in Keyes' possession at the time of his capture: Koenig's ATM card and cell phone (with the battery removed), a ski-mask, handgun, and bundles of rubber-banded cash that was traced to the recent National Bank of Texas robbery.

The authorities still had hope that Samantha was still alive.

But Keyes would tell them nothing. He stared straight ahead without emotion as detectives hammered him with questions. Authorities would get very little out of him. He was thirty-four years old and lived a quiet life with his girlfriend and ten year old daughter in Anchorage. Everything about Keyes' past seemed normal. But he had a creepy withdrawn nature about his personality. When the FBI searched his property, they found out why.

He had searched numerous time on his computer for Samantha Koenig. The FBI would then confront Keyes with the surveillance footage they had of his truck pulling up in front of the kiosk.

"We know it was your truck," the FBI agent said.

Keyes would remain silent for about forty seconds before he finally spoke.

"Well, I might as well tell you everything. She's dead."

Keyes revealed that he had used a needle and thread to open up Samantha's eyes as she posed with the newspaper in the ransom photo.

Keyes would recount how he brought Samantha back to his home and tied her up. He had a glass of wine before he began verbally taunting Samantha by telling her what he was going to do to her. He then raped the victim and choked her to death.

Only twenty feet away, his live-in girlfriend and ten year old daughter were sleeping. They would wake up the following morning and he would join them at the breakfast table. Like turning a switch on-and-off, he spoke of taking his family on a cruise.

"It was apparent that neither his girlfriend or his daughter knew of his crimes," Orange said. "He would tell investigators that 'no one really knew him.'"

Shortly after Keyes' capture in Lufkin, he was then extradited to Alaska to stand trial for Koenig's murder. His trial was set for March 2013 and he was slated to be represented by federal defender Rich Curtner. Keyes was thirty-four years old at the time of his arrest.

Investigation

Israel Keyes was officially extradited to Alaska on March 26, 2012. Shortly after arriving at the Anchorage Correctional Complex, Keyes confessed to the murder of Samantha Koenig, providing information which allowed investigators to locate her dismembered body on April 1st of the same year.

Keyes was initially willing to cooperate with authorities and offered to confess and plead guilty to all charges leveled against him if two terms were met: his trial would last no longer than one year and he would be given the death penalty. He also conditioned his cooperation on the basis that his name and certain details not be released to the media and public.

"I'm not in this for the glory," Keyes told interrogators. "I'm not trying to be on TV. I want my kid to have a chance to grow up. She's in a safe place now, she's not going to see any of this. I want her to have a chance to grow up and not have this hanging over her head."

In June 2012, Keyes attempted to violently escape from a courthouse in Anchorage, in what authorities suspected was a spur-of-the-moment suicide attempt. Keyes was successfully subdued with a taser and taken back into custody alive. Following his attempted escape, Keyes was placed on a suicide watch, which entailed a prohibition on razor blades and sharp objects, regular inspections of his cell, and a 24/7 guard.

The next month, in July 2012, a local news station, WCAX, reported Keyes' connection to the kidnapping and murder of the Curriers. This lead to Keyes ending all cooperation with the authorities for the next two months.

Modus Operandi

While cooperating with authorities at the Anchorage Correctional Complex, Keyes described his approach to killing thusly: "I would let them come to me... You might not get exactly what you're looking for, there's not much to pick from, so to speak. But there's also no witnesses, there's nobody else around."

Location

Israel Keyes was very methodical in his approach to killing. Unlike most serial killers, Keyes did not kill victims who lived near him. Most serial killers conduct most of their kidnapping and abductions within the vicinity of their home, which leads to an easier investigation and higher chance of being captured. Keyes, on the other hand, was known to take cross-country trips in order to kill.

For example, Keyes killed the Curriers in Vermont while he was living in Washington state. Once he decided to kill, Keyes booked a flight from Washington to Indiana. He then rented a car, removed the battery from his cell phone, and paid for all of his expenses with cash as he drove 1,000 miles to the East Coast. He tested his homemade silencer in New York, retrieved a murder toolkit that he had hidden in Vermont two years earlier, and then identified the Curriers as his next victims. This type of careful planning, attention to detail, and restraint is very uncommon in serial killers.

Victim Profile

Unlike most serial killers, Keyes did not have a specific victim profile. For instance, Ted Bundy, another serial killer who shared many qualities with Keyes, was known to target young, white women between the ages of 15 and 25. However, Keyes had no such victim profile. He alternatively killed or attempted to kill married couples, young woman, men, and several other unknown victims. This allowed him to operate without substantial police scrutiny for some time.

Method of Killing

With the exception of his killing of Bill Currier, Keyes strangled every one of his victims. Furthermore, Bill Currier was shot to death while attempting to escape from the house that Keyes was keeping him and his wife at. Had Bill not been killed in the heat of passion while attempting to escape, it is likely that Keyes eventually would have strangled him to death as well.

Death

After accidentally being provided with razors while on suicide watch, Keyes committed suicide on December 2nd, 2012. He sliced his wrists vertically and hung himself while being held at the Anchorage Correctional Complex. He was pronounced dead immediately.

Prior to committing suicide, Keyes composed a four-page, handwritten letter that was found underneath his body. The letter was covered in blood and was largely illegible, but FBI forensic investigators were able to reconstruct much of his letter.

While the letter did not provide additional details about his crimes and victims, it did offer a glimpse into his psyche and reasons for committing murders. Keyes wrote "Family and friends will shed a few tears, pretend it's off to heaven you go. But the reality is you were just bones and meat, and with your brain died also your soul." Later in his letter he elaborated, "You may have been free, you loved living your lie, fate had its own scheme crushed like a bug, you still die." He repeatedly referred to his victims as a "pretty captive butterfly."

Dr. Stephen Montgomery, a forensic psychiatrist at Vanderbilt University Medical Center analyzed the letter and reached the following conclusion: "It has no remorse, no regard for human life or the victims and that fits with that type of psychopathic personality."

Authorities are still investigating various unsolved disappearances throughout the various states that Keyes visited. It is now believed that he may have targeted homeless shelters where he could kill people who would not be missed.

RAILROAD KILLER

They called him the 'Railroad Killer.'

Angel Resendiz earned the nickname because of his penchant for committing his crimes near railroads, using the rail cars as his own personal get-away system.

Committing murder after murder, he was able to elude both American and Mexican authorities for over a decade.

EARLY LIFE

A birth certificate found by the FBI listed his date of birth as August 1st, 1960. He was born To Virginia de Maturino in the town of Izucar de Matomoros in the state of Puebla, Mexico. His mother has stated adamantly that the correct spelling of his surname is Recendis not Resendiz although the killer would have over fifty different aliases throughout his lifetime.

Angel had spent his childhood years with relatives and not with his immediate family. According to his mother, he was sexually abused by an uncle and other pedophiles in the town of Puebla. He would spend his youth roaming the streets, robbing, stealing and sniffing glue. Relatives would later testify that Resendiz was routinely beaten as a child, one time being "jumped" by several other youths who beat him so bad that he bled through his ears. Resendiz would leave home for months at a time then suddenly return mumbling about a coming religious apocalypse.

Legal trouble came early for Resendiz as he was caught trying to sneak into the Texas border at the age of sixteen. This would become the first of numerous run-ins with border patrol agents until he finally made it into the United States, making his way to St. Louis and finding work with a manufacturing company under an assumed name. He even registered to vote with his false identification.

In September of 1979, at the age of nineteen, Resendiz was arrested for assault and car theft in Miami. He was tried and sentenced to twenty-years in prison but was released after only six years and sent back to Mexico.

But he wouldn't stay there for long.

Through numerous attempts of trial and error, Resendiz had learned not only to game the system but to enter and exit the United States with minimal detection.

He learn to use the rail-cars...

AN "INVISIBLE" MAN

Resendiz became so skilled at crossing the border without detection that he began charging for his services. He began to make a living as a human smuggler, transporting Mexicans across the border for a fee.

Resendiz soon developed a reputation for his smuggling skills, often being seen as a 'go to' person in his Ciudad Juarez neighborhood called 'Patria.'

He would make weekly crossings over the border, being arrested only intermittently. He would then be deported back into his native land only to ping-pong back and forth.

Finally, Resendiz would serve prison terms for his crimes. He would be arrested in Texas for false identity and citizenship, getting a year and half worth of jail.

Upon release in 1987, he journeyed to New Orleans and was arrested for carrying a concealed weapon. He received another year and half worth of prison time until parole.

He then went back to his old haunts in St. Louis where he tried to defraud Social Security and receive illegal payments. He got caught and served a three year sentence.

Resendiz then decided small-time burglaries were his deal. He once again illegally crossed the border, journeyed to New Mexico and was caught burglarizing a home. He was imprisoned for eighteen months and upon release he broke into a Santa Fe rail yard, being captured yet again.

"They should have called Resendiz the boomerang man," forensic psychologist Frank Lizzo said. "He knew how to play the game and seemingly had no fear of the system. The system never punished him severely enough for him to stop his crimes, let alone stop crossing the border."

After his last recorded deportation, the killings began.

THE KILLING FIELDS

"He probably started killing somewhere in his late 20s," Douglas said. "He may have killed people like himself initially – males, transients...(he) became angry at the population at large. What America represents here is this wealthy country where he keeps getting kicked out...(he) just can't make ends meet. Coupled with these feelings, these inadequacies, fueled by the fact that he's known to take alcohol, take drugs, lowers his inhibitions now to go out and kill."

Angel's list of victims began in 1986. Continuing to bounce in and out of the United States, he shot a homeless woman and left her for dead in an abandoned farm house. He had met the acquaintance of the woman at a homeless shelter and they became friends. They would later take a trip on a motorcycle together when he felt that the woman disrespected him.

Resendiz would then take out his gun and blow her head off.

The woman allegedly had a boyfriend whom Resendiz shot and killed as well. He said that he dumped his body in a creek between San Antonio and Uvalde. This killing has never been verified aside from what Resendiz revealed to the police during his interrogation sessions.

Five years later, Resendiz would kill Michael White because he was a "homosexual." Resendiz would bludgeon White to death with a brick and leave him in front of an abandoned home.

These were seemingly warm-ups for the more brutal crimes to come which would also include rape.

"Sex seemed almost secondary," FBI profiler John Douglas said when apprised of Resendiz's crimes. "(He is) just a bungling crook ...very disorganized."

Douglas would later concede, however, that it was this disorganization that worked in his favor. Like a true drifter, Resendiz' whereabouts became as elusive as a rational thought in his head.

"When he hitches a ride on the freight train, he doesn't necessarily know where the train is going," Douglas said. "But when he gets off, having background as a burglar, he's able to scope out the area, do a little surveillance, make sure he breaks into the right house where there won't be anyone to give him a run for his money. He can enter a home complete with cutting glass and reaching in and undoing the locks."

"He'll look through the windows and see who's occupying it. The guy's only 5 foot-7, very small. In fact...the early weapons were primarily blunt-force trauma weapons, weapons of opportunity found at the scenes. He has to case them out, make sure he can put himself in a win-win situation."

Resendiz would also leave his weapon of choice up to chance. Whatever the home would have, a statue a mantle piece, a butcher knife, that would become the instrument of murder.

FLORIDA KILLINGS

On March 23rd, 1997, Jesse Howell would be found bludgeoned to death beside the railroad tracks in Ocala, Florida. He was nineteen years old.

"When we got there," Sheriff Patty Lumpkin said. "We see what appears to be a young male, in his late teens or early twenties. Blood around the head area. You could tell by looking at him that he was dead. The first thing I do is make sure that we've got our forensics people on the way, on the medical examiners on the way, and all the investigators that we have called out or either there or en route."

"When those types of things happen it might have been someone who had fallen off a train," Lt. Jeff Owens said. "Or someone who could have been struck by a train."

The authorities quickly ruled out an accident, however, as they examined the body.

"It didn't appear to be an accident," Lumpkin said. "Because if he had been hit by the train the trauma would have been much more extreme. I've seen some deaths from trains and the initial impact from the train would have done more harm to the body."

The forensic team did determine that Howell's body looked as if he were the victim of blunt force trauma.

"We did see a baseball type of cap," forensic scientist Michael Dunn said. "It appeared to have blood on the inside surface of he bill. In addition, there was a pair of wire rimmed eye glasses and one of the eye pieces was missing, one of the lenses was out. This didn't look good either. As we moved closer, we saw that the victim had been dragged to that spot using just the blue jean material around the cuff (of his pants)."

Near the body, they found a brass and rubber coupling. This device was used to link one train car to another. It could also be used as a clubbing weapon.

"It had what appeared to be blood on it (the coupling)," Dunn recalled.

Howell still had jewelry on his person. He wore a gold cross necklace, a watch and a small amount of cash in his pocket. The police ruled out robbery as a motive.

The police did not identify Howell's body right off the bat. They did find a money wire receipt where some money had been wired from Illinois to Florida. The name on the receipt was of a woman named "Wendy."

Police tracked the money transfer to its point of origin which was all the way in Woodstock, Illinois.

Coincidentally, the authorities there were investigating the disappearance of Wendy Von Huben.

Wendy was missing alongside her boyfriend, the nineteen year old Jesse Howell.

"They advised me that they were investigating a John Doe," Woodstock Detective Kurt Rosenquest recalled. "Unidentified male."

Rosenquest then followed up with the investigating team in Florida, sending them the fingerprints and pictures of Jesse Howell.

The Ocala police would then positively identify Howell.

Jesse had met Wendy only months earlier. They had secretly planned to marry and went on a road trip with another couple.

The other couple, however, grew tired of Jesse and Wendy's constant bickering. They demanded to be let out of the car and left. Jesse and Wendy continued into Ocala, Florida where they ran out of money.

Wendy would call her parents in Illinois who would then transfer her $200 via Western Union. The couple would collect the $200 but would not return home.

"We checked Greyhounds," Rosenquest said. "Nobody matching their description ordered buses or train tickets back to the Woodstock area."

Tears were shed as Rosenquest informed Howell's parents that their teen son had been murdered. The investigative team then turned their attention to the disappearance of Wendy.

They held out hope because there were issues between her and Jesse, thinking that perhaps she simply ran off to be by herself.

Police scoured the surrounding areas and used helicopters in all directions around the railroad tracks.

They would find nothing. There was no DNA left behind on Jesse Howell's body either.

Papers and fliers with Wendy Von Huben's information was distributed all throughout Florida up through Illinois.

Authorities also began interviewing the transient population that lived along the railroad tracks.

Two and a half months later, however, Wendy's parents would receive a phone call.

"The phone rang," Rosenquest recalled. "Wendy's father answered the phone. The girl was crying. She said 'I'm sorry. I love you.'"

She would tell the father she was two hours away from Woodstock at a gas station. The father asked for the phone number on the pay phone she was calling from and she said that there wasn't any before hanging up.

The police were not certain that the phone call came from Wendy so they immediately headed out to the gas station where they believe the call took place.

Police tracked down the surveillance video of the gas station. On the video, a woman that physically resembled Wendy entered the gas station.

The phone records, however, revealed that the call did not come from the gas station where the surveillance video revealed a woman who allegedly was Wendy. It came from another gas station where there were fliers posted of Wendy.

Someone had played a cruel hoax as Wendy's parents had added their home number to the fliers

ONE-LEGGED BOB AND A CHANCE DISCOVERY

A year went by without any sign of Wendy.

There was some ray of hope, however, as the railroad authorities called the Ocala police and informed them that the received information from a member of one of the homeless camps. They had a man in custody named "One Legged Bob" who was traveling with a girl and may be responsible for the murder of her previous boyfriend.

"'One Legged Bob' was your typical homeless person," Owens said. "Kinda scruffy. Hadn't shaved in a few days. He had a prosthetic leg that helped him get around. For someone who you might consider crippled, he was far from crippled."

Owens would spend the next eight hours interviewing the only lead he had, a one legged homeless man.

After the grueling interrogation, Owens realized that he had the wrong suspect.

By sheer chance, however, Patty Lumpkin heard about someone they dubbed the "Railroad Killer" during a class she was taking at the FBI.

"They called him the Railway Killer," Lumpkin recalled. "The Angel of Death. He was killing people. Leaving them near the railroad or he was killing them at homes or locations that were close to the railroad.

The FBI knew the Railway Killer as Angel Resendiz.

"We knew that Angel Resendiz was a person that rode the rails across the country," FBI Agent Mark Young said. "We were worried where he'd wind up next. So we decided to make him a top ten fugitive. Maybe the millions of eyes of the public would tell us something."

The strategy worked.

"He was one of the most vile, evil persons that I had ever dealt with," Young said. "It was like every time you turn around there's another murder."

Owens and Lumpkin hoped to talk to Resendiz to query him about Jesse Howell's murder and Wendy Von Huben's disappearance.

"The attorneys representing him at the time in Texas stopped us," Owens said. "They wanted to protect their client from talking. Any defense attorney who represents a criminal will generally tell the person to stop talking to law enforcement."

Resendiz was placed on death row and Texas had a fast execution rate. The two detectives worried that they would lose their chance to interview Resendiz and connect him to the crimes in Ocala.

Owens and Lumpkin decided to mail Resendiz a letter, respectfully asking him if they could interview him. The letter was written in a formal manner and even addressed him as "Senor."

To their surprise, Resendiz responded back and granted them an interview regarding his involvement in Jesse's killing and Wendy's disappearance.

During their meeting, Resendiz was quick to admit that he had killed Jesse. The detectives deliberately withheld information about the killing, holding back details that only the killer would know. But when Resendiz described using a brake coupling from one of the trains, they knew they had their killer.

But they needed to find out what happened to Wendy.

In a follow-up letter, they promised him immunity from prosecution if he agreed to talk. It was a moot point by then as he was already on death row but the detectives still needed permission from Wendy's family to go through with the interview.

In order to receive some sense of closure, the family agreed to the immunity.

"When we get to the prison," Lumpkin said. "We see him coming down the hallway. He (Resendiz) has a waist belt on. It's an electric shock belt and he's chained to the belt. He's just a mild-mannered person but remember that a psychopath or a sociopath doesn't have any feeling. I mean he had dead eyes. He had no feeling in that body. He didn't care about anything."

Resendiz would reveal that he was heading south for work when the train stopped and he spotted Jesse getting off the train for a smoke.

"Resendiz told us that he killed Jesse with a piece of the train coupling," Lumpkin said. "And Wendy was asleep on the train when this took place. And then when they went down the road further somehow he talked Wendy into getting off the train."

Resendiz then raped and strangled Wendy to death.

Resendiz drew a map of where had left Wendy's body. He described burying her in a shallow grave near a canopy of trees. Resendiz would remember that she had a book in a back pack and an army style jacket that he used to cover her fresh grave.

Police would return to the site and were able to locate where he buried Wendy's body. Almost three years after the murder, everything the killer described was still there. The book. The jacket.

And Wendy's body.

"When Wendy ran away she had a small engagement ring," Owen said. "And she had a Winnie the Pooh wristwatch.

The detective would bring those items back to Wendy's parents.

KENTUCKY RAILROAD MURDER

In August of 1997, Resendiz would make his way from Ocala, Florida to Lexington, Kentucky. It was there he would stalk two young college students.

Holly Dunn was a 20-year old junior at the University of Kentucky and it was there she met Christopher Maier.

"Chris Maier was my very good friend," Dunn recalled. "He was just the nicest, kindest man. We decided that we wanted to be more than friends then we started dating. We dated for about three months."

"Chris and I were attending a party. We decided that the party wasn't very fun so we went to go talk a walk by the railroad tracks. We sat down and talked for awhile and when we got up to leave a man came out from behind an electrical box. He had a weapon that he used on Chris. It was some sort of ice pick or screw driver. Something sharp. I guess our immediate thought was he's going to rob us. That's when we realize he wants money we start thinking 'okay, well, you could have our credit card, you can have our ATM card, you can have our car.' Then he started tying up Chris' hands behind his back. And then he came over to me and he took off my belt and that's when I started thinking he doesn't want to rob us."

After tying up Holly, Resendiz then pulled Chris by the shirt across the railroad tracks and into a ditch.

Holly would follow on her knees, pleading for him to stop whatever he was about to do.

"Lie down," Resendiz said, his voice soft but menacing.

"Everything is going to be okay," Christopher said to Holly as Resendiz dragged him into the ditch.

"Shut up!" Resendiz commanded as he gagged Christopher with a sock.

Resendiz then walked off into the darkness. The frightened couple did not know what the psychopath had planned.

"Then he comes with this rock," Holly recalled. "There was no warning, he drops this rock on Chris' head. I'm just thinking 'what just happened?' I don't even know what just happened."

"You don't have to worry about him anymore," Resendiz said to Holly as he got on top of her.

"I went into survival mode, I'm thinking, I mean he's gonna kill me. I may as well fight. I'm gonna fight. He unties my feet and climbs on top of me. I start to kick and scream and hit him but he held that knife or ice pick (to my throat) and said 'look how easily I could kill you.' I stopped everything and then he raped me."

"I memorized his face," Dunn said. "I stared at him and memorized, he had a tattoo on his arm, I was thinking if you have any scars I'm gonna remember your scars, I'm gonna remember your face,I'm not gonna forget it because if I live through this I will get you."

Resendiz completed the sexual assault of Dunn before smashing her head with a rock.

"He hit me five or six times in my face," Dunn recalled. "I think I put my hand up and then I turned over and then he hit me five or six times in the back of my head. He hit me hard. He was trying to kill me. I think I laid there and he thought I was dead."

Resendiz did think she was did as he threw the rock down and ran away from the crime scene.

Holly would suffer severe facial trauma but miraculously survived the attack.

"I had a broken jaw," Dunn said. "Broken eye socket and cuts on the back of my head that they had to staple shut and then I had cuts on my face."

She woke up in a Kentucky hospital, surrounded by family members.

"Everyone was told not to talk about Chris to me. I just said 'Chris is dead, isn't he?' And my Dad actually is the one I said that to and he was like 'yes, he died.'"

TEXAS TERROR

Resendiz would travel to Texas via train and in October of 1988 he flopped down in Hughes Springs. He would enter the home of 87-year old Leafie Mason, attacking the woman with an iron and killing her.

Two months later, Resendiz would sneak into the home of Dr. Claudia Benton, a thirty-nine year old medical researcher who lived in a suburb of Houston near the railroad tracks.

Again, it was a case of a home being to close to the train tracks. The train would provide the perfect cover for the sneaky Resendiz as he realized that the sound of the rail-car racing by would allow him to break in homes without being heard.

He applied the same technique with Benton, breaking into her home, raping then killing her.

Police would find the doctor face down on the floor. Her bedroom soaked in blood, ransacked for any valuables.

He head had been covered in a plastic bag while her body had been covered in a blanket.

"It appears that she (Claudia Benton) was sleeping," recalled Ken Macha, former police sergeant. "He was able to get in and picked up a bronze statuette from the mantle in the living room. He was relentless in beating her. The skull fractures themselves would have been enough to kill her. She was then stabbed in the back with a very large butcher knife."

"Resendiz was brutal, sadistic," said former West University police chief Gary Brye.

Fingerprints and DNA evidence would link Resendiz to the crime.

The problem was they could catch the man that Texas Ranger Drew Carter referred to as "a walking, breathing form of evil."

EVADING POLICE

Seven months later, Resendiz would continue to avoid capture. He remained in Texas, riding the rail cars until coming into the town of Weimar. He would break into the home of Pastor Norman "Skip" Sirnic and his wife Karen. Resendiz smashed a jack hammer into both of their heads, killing them instantly. He would then rape the body of Karen postmortem.

"He would watch these places," prosecuting attorney Devin Anderson said. "He would watch them, wait for them to go to sleep, get in their house and he would strike them before they would even wake up. I thought we have got to catch this guy."

The DNA found at the scene of the Sirnic murders would match those left on Benton. The FBI then realized they had a highly mobile serial killer on the loose...someone who could kill in one town then appear in another town miles away and kill again.

Resendiz was also smart. He would constantly alter his appearance. He'd shave his head. Then his mustache. He'd be clean shaven one week. Unkempt the next. He would wear glasses one week. No glasses the next.

Authorities could not get an accurate description of him other than the fact that he was small.

Resendiz was also able to take advantage of the lack of a coordinated computer system that gave law enforcement the ability to cross-check fugitives. After the Sirnic murders, Border Patrol had encountered Resendiz near the El Paso border but did not find him on the wanted list.

They then deported him back to Mexico.

Within 48 hours, Resendiz was back across the border to resume his killing spree.

"Our computers told us that he was nothing of lookout material," said C.G. Almengor, a supervisor at the border."We really wish he had been in the system so we could have caught him."

Resendiz would be deported no less than seventeen times over the course of his rampage. At no point did authorities make the connection because of his changing appearance, use of different aliases and the lack of a connected system to document illegals trying to come across the border.

A PREFERENCE FOR TEXAS

Noemi Dominguez was a graduate of Rice University who had just recently quit her job as an elementary school teacher to pursue a master's degree.

She was described as "the sweetest, nicest teacher – a darling who went the extra mile."

Fueled by hate, Resendiz would break into Noemi's home and rape her before killing her with a pick ax. He then stole her car and drove to Schulenberg, Texas where he would kill Josephine Konvicka with the same pick ax.

He would leave the weapon embedded in Konvicka's head as well as leave his fingerprints all over the home. He was more than just sloppy, he was getting cocky. He left a newspaper article that described his crimes as well as a toy train...a reference to his nickname as the "Railroad Killer."

Resendiz was also meticulous in approaching his victims.

"He undid the light in her (Noemi's) car," Anderson said. "So when he opened the door it wouldn't come on. That's who were were dealing with. Someone who really knew how to sneak around. Who really knew how to avoid detection."

"He kept killing people. He would not stop. In his mode of transportation, using the railroads was brilliant because they couldn't be monitored. I mean there's thousands of trains and millions of miles of tracks all over the United States."

"I felt hopeless at the time. Because if you're willing to sleep in a train or you're willing to sleep in a field, you can stay lost for a long, long time and I didn't think we were ever going to catch him."

Later that month, Resendiz had journeyed to Illinois, reaching the town of Gorham. He would break into the home of 80-year old George Morber and his daughter Carolyn Frederick. Resendiz would tie Morber to a chair and shoot him in the back of the head with a shotgun. He then raped Carolyn and smashed the shotgun across her head with such force that the weapon broke in half.

Both Morber and Frederick would die from their injuries.

The FBI placed him on their Top Ten list.

They then recruited his common-law wife, Julietta Reyes, and brought her into Houston for questioning from her hometown of Rodeo, Mexico.

Reyes complied with police requests, turning over over ninety-three pieces of jewelry that her husband had mailed to her from the U.S.

Relatives of Noemi Dominguez claimed thirteen pieces. George Benton was able to identify some pieces of jewelry as belonging to his wife as well.

Police would then locate Resendiz's half-sister, Manuela Karkiewicz, who lived in New Mexico. Initially, she refused to cooperate. She worried that the FBI or the police would kill her brother. But Carter convinced her to talk Resendiz into giving himself up.

The FBI knew that Resendiz had made his way back to Mexico after the murders in Illinois and was hiding in his hometown neighborhood of Patria.

Carter was able to get a rapport with Manuela. He convinced her that Resendiz would receive "personal safety while in jail, regular visiting rights for his family and a psychological evaluation."

"I came away with the impression that they (Resendiz' family) definitely had an understanding of right and wrong ... and knew now that what Maturino Resendiz was accused of doing was heinous and wrong ... ," Carter said. "Manuela, especially, came across as a woman of strong faith. There was a very deep emotional strain and burden placed on her in this investigation. She had to make some very difficult choices that impacted her and her family. And, in the end, her actions alone speak to her character."

Carter spent weeks talking to Manuela who in turn "worked a miracle."

They got the serial killer to surrender.

On July 12th, Manuela would receive a fax from the district attorney's office in Harris County which formalized everything that Texas Ranger Carter had promised.

The word passed from Manuela to another relative who acted as a go-between with Resendiz. The relative than came back later that evening and said that Resendiz would surrender in the morning at 9 a.m.

Texas Ranger Drew Carter would accompany Manuela and a spiritual adviser to meet with Resendiz on a bridge that connected El Paso, Texas to Ciudad Juarez.

"When I saw that face there was a little bit of excitement there because I finally said, 'This is going to happen,'" Carter recalled as he remembered Resendiz appearing on the bridge with his dirty jeans, muddy boots and blank facial expression. "He stuck out his hand, I stuck out my hand, and we shook hands."

Resendiz would then surrender to the Texas Ranger.
DEATH PENALTY
Resendiz' attorneys knew that their only hope would be an insanity defense. The Mexican government also got involved, lobbying authorities to spare Resendiz the death penalty

"Insanity was the logical defense because no one wants to believe that there is someone out there who would do things like that," Anderson said. "That was the thing that worried me the most about the case was that jurors would just throw up their hands and say nobody in their right mind could do what he does."

"The thing about what a life sentence with Resendiz would have been, he would have enjoyed it. I mean he would have had pen pals. He would have given interviews if they let him, I mean he would have loved it. And I knew that. And he didn't deserve to live after what he did just didn't. He caused so much pain, so much heartache and so much terror, that's what the whole focus of the trial had to be."

George Benton, the husband of Claudia, would vehemently criticize the Mexican government who support his appeals and domestic opposition to the death penalty.

"(He)looked like a man and walked like a man. But what lived within that skin was not a human being."

"He was small," Anderson said when she first saw Resendiz in the courtroom. "Maybe five- foot five. His forearms though, were roped with muscles. He was scary. Even though he was small you could feel he was dangerous. He looked like a wild animal who'd been caught."

Resendiz looked "timid" in the courtroom and spoke of himself in religious riddles. He claimed he was Jewish and didn't seem effected when he was informed that the prosecution was aiming for the death penalty.

"I don't believe in death," Resendiz, said. "I know the body is going to go to waste. But me, as a person, I'm eternal. I'm going to be alive forever."

The defense said that Resendiz' crimes were caused by head injuries, drug abuse and a family history of mental illness. He has a delusional perception of the world as he believes that he can cause earthquakes, floods, and explosions and that God told him to kill his victims whom they believed to be evil.

He made a living stealing things from his victims and having his wife sell them in Mexico. "That was his job," Anderson said. "And for recreation it was killing the people who lived in the house."

"He was a very intelligent person who worked the system and knew exactly what kinds of things to say to get that defense to work."

The jury, however, would find Resendiz guilty after one hour and forty-five minutes of deliberation.

He was sentenced to die via lethal injection.

"He made it very clear during my conversation with him that he deserves to die," Owens said.

"I want to ask if it is in your heart to forgive me," Resendiz said in his final words. "You don't have to. I know I allowed the devil to rule my life. I just ask you to forgive me and ask the Lord to forgive me for allowing the devil to deceive me. I thank God for having patience with me. I don't deserve to cause you pain. You did not deserve this. I deserve what I am getting."

Resendiz then prayed in Hebrew and Spanish before drawing his final breath.

THE CAMDEN RIPPER

DWIGHT HALL

Whitechapel, London was not a safe place for women in the 1880's, as an unknown man was killing prostitutes throughout the region, and police had no idea who this mystery person was. He was eventually dubbed 'Jack the Ripper', but his real identity was never discovered. Just over a hundred years later London became precarious once again as Anthony Hardy, a man who has been obsessed with Jack the Ripper for most of his life, took to the streets to emulate his hero. Hardy was eventually given the name 'the Camden Ripper', but this time, police are on to his game.

Anthony Hardy was born on May 31, 1951, to parents in a working-class suburb of London. His father was a miner and worked hard to support his wife and five children. According to many, Hardy's childhood in Burton upon Trent was unremarkable.

"He seems to have been an uncomplicated child. A bit quiet, a bit of a loner," said Dr. Jane Monkton Smith, criminologist

Often times, experts point to a traumatic event in childhood to explain a serial killer's motives for becoming so twisted, but Hardy experienced nothing traumatic growing up, the only negative in his life was his embarrassment at being born into a lower class family.

Hardy was a remarkably bright child. He excelled in school. Although he was expected to follow in his father's footsteps and become a miner, Hardy had bigger, more important dreams for himself.

"His father was a miner and they were from the lower middle class, which he didn't like," said Smith.

Nigel Weir, senior police detective, explained why Hardy was so desperate to separate himself from his low-class family; "it was normal that you would follow your father, so it was expected that Anthony would go down the mines. He obviously wanted to choose something better for himself."

Hardy worked hard to improve his prospects. After he finished primary and high school, Hardy went on to attend Imperial College in London, a very prestigious school where he studied engineering.

Hardy's intelligence would later become a key characteristic, and would shape the unspeakable crimes he would commit as an adult.

Even at this young age, Hardy was beginning to believe few people, if any, could match his level of intelligence.

Weir explained Hardy's internal thoughts at this time as, " 'I'm cleverer than you,' that is what would come out of this, because at the end of the day, academically, he was cleverer," said Weir.

Throughout college Hardy continued to distinguish himself as a bright individual. He soon realized he also had a way with the women on campus, who were attracted to his brains and his looks.

In 1972, while he was still attending school, Hardy married Judith Dwight. She was his equal in both intelligence and looks, and from the outside, it seemed as if the two were a perfect match.

"She was obviously his equal in terms of intellectual achievement and understanding, and they appeared a fine match," said Colin Sutton, metropolitan police officer.

Once he graduated from college, Hardy began working for British Sugar. It was a prestigious job and one which helped Hardy move out of the lower class once and for all, or so he thought.

Things were good for the young couple, so they decided it was time to start a family, and soon four children were born. Happiness didn't last long for the Hardy's however. The stress of such a high profile job was hard on Hardy, and the rest of the family and Hardy began to show a violent nature towards his wife.

"What I think is pretty clear looking at the history of their relationship, that it wasn't just a little bit of domestic violence," said Smith. "Anthony Hardy was pretty much what we would call a stereotypical abuser."

Sutton also offers a chilling detail about Hardy's inclination towards violence, "the predisposition to extreme violence will often be accompanied by a willingness to use violence against your loved ones," he said.

Looking back, it's hard not to wonder if authorities had noticed the violence early in Hardy's life, could they have stopped this man from becoming the horrifying killer known as the Camden Ripper?

As well as becoming habitually violent, Hardy began traveling with his job around this time, and established a lifelong addiction to sex, anyway, he could get it. He began to have a number of extramarital affairs with prostitutes. He didn't even try to hide the secret from his wife, or anyone else. Hardy's hero, Jack the Ripper was known for having relationships with prostitutes as well.

"A number of prostitutes came forward to say they had encountered him," said Steve Bird, crime reporter. "A lot of them gave harrowing accounts of how violent he was during the sex act. Some of them said they were unable to breathe while he had sex with them. Others claimed that he was just incredibly violent and seemed to be into sadomasochism."

In the mid-1970's life is not great for the Hardy family, but things are about to get worse, the working class boy who had worked hard to transform his fortunes lost his job. It's not his fault, just an economic downturn. But, Hardy begins to suffer from depression and mood swings and doctors prescribed him medication. Today he would be diagnosed as bipolar, a condition still uncategorized at the time, and one which can lead to exceptionally violent behavior. The diagnosis is the start of a mental illness which will shape his life forever, and end the lives of others he encounters along the way.

Instead of going down in the mines, Hardy took a job halfway across the world in Tasmania, Australia in the late 1970's. It should have been a fresh start for the family, but instead, things only got worse from there.

"The family was very excited about the move to Tasmania, it sounds very exotic, a place where the family could consider themselves starting fresh," said Bird.

If the family was hoping for a fresh start in a new place, they were sadly mistaken, Hardy's desire for sex outside of his marriage was just as strong as it was in London. It was later established while in Tasmania Hardy still had affairs, still visited prostitutes, still abused his wife. He became more controlling over every aspect of his life.

"The group of men who are particularly dangerous, and the group of men who serially commit domestic violence are usually incredibly controlling individuals," said Smith, "and Anthony Hardy was one of those individuals."

Hardy was not able to keep his new job for long. In 1986, for the second time, Hardy was let go in a round of job cuts.

As Hardy's life spun even more out of control, he became more violent. Hardy's marriage wasn't working, he was clinically depressed, and had yet again been thrown out of a job. Throughout this time, he had maintained a fascination with Jack the Ripper. He read books about the mysterious killer on a regular basis. But, while the 19th-century slaughterer used crude methods to kill, Hardy chose a more devious means for his first attempt at murder. The victim, his wife.

"He tried to create a perfect crime," said Bird. "He actually used his scientific knowledge to be able to carry out a crime that he hoped would be undetectable."

Hardy filled a water bottle full of water and then froze it. As the bottle was freezing, Hardy drew a bath. Once everything was ready, Hardy took the frozen water bottle from his freezer and went to find his sleeping wife. He beat her over the head repeatedly with the bottle. Once she was severely injured, and semi-conscious, Hardy planned to put her in the bathtub. Later, when the authorities found her, Hardy assumed they would rule her death an accidental drowning because it would look as if she had been knocked unconscious after slipping while entering the tub. In the meantime, his murder weapon would melt, and he could dispose of all the evidence. Hardy thought he would never be discovered, just like his hero, Jack the Ripper.

"The amount of planning is quite unusual, that he would plan that far in advance," said Smith.

One thing Hardy didn't count on in his plan was his wife making noise as he was beating her. She was so loud, she woke up their young children at one point, who came into the room to see what was going on. The authorities were called before any serious damage could be done, and Judith escaped from certain death.

"Hardy didn't care the effect it [his attack] had on his child, it was just part and parcel of him getting his own way," said Bird.

Hardy was arrested after the attack on his wife, but he wasn't worried.

"He confessed to it and said he had actually fully intended to kill her that night. This was a very, very dangerous man," said Smith.

Anthony Hardy had exhibited a taste for the sort of brutality used by Jack the Ripper. He now faced jail time for attempted murder. But, this was in an era when domestic violence was dealt with differently than today, and his crime was considered just that, domestic violence.

"Their view was in 1970's Australia, the same as 1970's England; it's a domestic, it stays at home," said Weir.

Hardy knew he was smarter than any police officer, and he would be able to talk his way out of this situation. He soon convinced the police he was mentally unstable and he didn't need jail time, he needed to spend time in a mental hospital until he could recover his senses. The police agreed and he was sent to a hospital to be evaluated by psychologists.

Hardy told a friend, Maureen Reeves, years later going into the mental hospital was all an act to fool people for whom he had no respect.

"He said that, 'they're not very intelligent because they couldn't catch Jack the Ripper.' " Reeves said. "With the psychologists, he said, 'they're not very clever people.' And I said, 'well they must be because that's their job, you know, to help people.' He said, 'no, you can tell them things and they sometimes just agree with you.' But he always said he could beat a psychologist."

Inside the psychiatric unit in Queensland Hardy cooperated with staff, he took his medication, he played the game with just one intention, to get out as quickly as possible.

"He evaded, what otherwise would have been perhaps a pretty stiff sentence for a crime of attempted murder," said Sutton.

After a few months in the hospital, Hardy was released. His family had returned to England while he was away, but because this is still the 1970's there is no restraining order in place, and Hardy was free to go back to England himself and stalk them.

"Even though he had tried to kill his wife, he returned to Britain an innocent man," said Smith.

After his release from the hospital, Hardy became even more dangerous.

"It's possible that Mr. Hardy believed that being released back into normal life, then he's beaten the system," said Weir. "He beat the police in Australia. As far as he's concerned, he's back. He's number one."

Judith called the police several times to report her ex-husband following her, but there is little that can be done to stop it.

"She would regularly contact police saying this guy was still after her," said Bird, "and he became increasingly sinister, increasingly menacing towards her."

It's around this time Hardy begins a normal friendship with Reeves. He keeps his dark past hidden from her, and she has no reason to suspect Hardy is hiding anything sinister, nor does she have any idea of the horrors her new friend will commit in the future. Hardy even talks to Reeves sometimes about his obsession with Jack the Ripper, but still, she doesn't think anything is out of the ordinary.

"No other person for ten years knew him how I knew him, and all the discussions we had about different things, alright yes he was obsessed with Jack the Ripper, but that to me is not unusual, some people are interested, some people are fascinated by him," said Reeves.

The family of Anthony Hardy is tormented for several months, Hardy himself becomes more intense with his threats and actions towards the family. Finally, Judith is able to get a restraining order put in place for her ex-husband. But, his need to control her is too great. He broke the restraining order and was punished with a short jail sentence.

"Stalkers are very often obsessive people," said Sutton. "Of course, obsessions can lead to behavior which is out of the ordinary and not what one would expect."

On his release from jail, Hardy decides to finally leave his old family alone. He moved on to easier and more vulnerable targets; prostitutes. Hardy moved to the Kings Cross area of London. Near Whitechapel, where it was just over a century before where Hardy's hero Jack the Ripper terrorized the streets and killed without mercy.

"Kings Cross at the time attracted a transient population, there was a major train station there," said Bird. "It was where prostitutes, pimps and drug dealers hanged out. For Hardy, this was an ideal place to live."

It seemed as if Hardy was given a fresh start in Kings Cross. The police in this area were not aware of his violent past, or the fact he had tried to kill his wife when they were living in Australia. To them, he was just another man obsessed with sex taking full advantage of what the prostitutes were offering in this area. Unfortunately, no one has any idea just how much danger these women are in.

"That's when you see a deterioration in not only the quality of his life but also in the quality of his mental state," said Sutton. "There seems to have been a spiral of deterioration involving drugs, involving alcohol and depression which lead him to the low point until the horror that we ultimately saw."

In the late 1990's Hardy was diagnosed with diabetes, a condition in which, in his case, caused impotence. This could have been the final straw to push this once high achiever to multiple murderer. Although he was now impotent, Hardy was still just as addicted to sex as before, so he began to seek out more devious, and more violent sex to satisfy his needs.

"For a man who's already violent, who already suffers rages perhaps, and who is already a misogynist, to then find that he cannot achieve satisfaction in the usual ways and has to go further and further that's going to be a problem," said Smith.

Anthony Hardy was now set on a road to destruction. The consequences seemed inevitable.

"He is a sadistic and controlling individual. He suffers with psychotic incidences," said Smith. "So, we've got a man who is not totally in control and who is, to put it in simple terms, a ticking time bomb."

The bomb is about to explode. Hardy was now living in a run-down area of London, filled with prostitutes, and degradation. He craved sex and drugs, and both were easy enough to get. His life, which once seemed so bright and full of promise was now in ruins and Hardy didn't seem to care. He would go for long periods of time without washing himself, or even changing his clothes. Hardy only had one thing on his mind now; violence. And he won't stop till get gets it.

Hardy still cultivates relationships with vulnerable prostitutes as often as he can, the encounters are just as violent as ever. In 1998, he went too far and a prostitute accused him of rape. How can Hardy escape justice this time?

"These crimes sometimes being difficult to prove, and certainly in 1998, and sometimes victims being unwilling to go through with it because the support perhaps wasn't there for them at the time," said Sutton. "It came to nothing in terms of the prosecution, but it came, we have a very serious indication, precursor, of how Hardy was prepared to treat women."

After the accusation, Hardy was arrested and questioned by the police. He was soon released, however, due to lack of evidence, and because the prostitute in question did not wish to testify in court. Once again, Hardy escaped justice. Once again, Hardy thought he was above the law. And once again, Hardy thought he was untouchable.

"He's thinking, 'I'm untouchable, I'm unalike, they're not going to get me,' " said Sutton.

It was around this time Hardy struck up a friendship with one of his neighbors, Alan Young. The two met in the courtyard of their apartment building and soon began chatting. Young had no idea just how dangerous the person he was talking to would turn out to be.

"We just had conversations, that's all. Just everyday topics, things like that, a bit of politics, bits of this that and the other. And that was it," said Young of how the two first met.

Hardy was careful not to reveal too much to his new friend and kept his darkest secrets deep inside.

The next few years passed in relative normalcy, but Hardy did not get along with all his neighbors as well as he did with Young. In 2002, the police were called to the apartment complex after a dispute between Hardy and one such neighbor got out of hand. To get back at a neighbor for her shower or bath supposedly dripping water in Hardy's apartment, he defaced her door with several obscenities, then he threw battery acid through her mail slot.

"It wasn't just simple criminal damage, this was really rather nasty abuse across the door and battery acid through the mail slot," said Smith. "They already knew that they were dealing with somebody who was potentially quite dangerous."

As police were investigating the incident they noticed a door in Hardy's apartment which was locked. They asked him for the key, and he responded by saying he didn't have one. The room was, according to Hardy, used by a border and he did not have access.

Police didn't question Hardy's story, but they asked him to grab a jacket and come with them down to the police station for further questioning. One quick look in the pockets of the jacket Hardy grabbed, and police found the key to open this door. What the police found behind the door was more shocking than they could ever have imagined.

"What they found then was obviously quite horrific for anybody to find," said Weir. "They found, lying on the bed, the naked body of a woman. We're thinking the worst, we're thinking suspicious, we're thinking has he killed this woman."

Earlier in the week, a sex worker named Sally Rose White had come into contact with Hardy while she was working the streets. Her colleagues would never see her again, they had no idea where she disappeared to after she was seen with Hardy, but they did know she was in great danger. White was born with a spinal injury which plagued her for most of her life, with both physical and mental disabilities. It was difficult for her to hold down any job, besides prostitution, and her drug addiction left her with no other choice. It was her body police stumbled upon when they opened the locked door in Hardy's apartment. She was dead.

"It must be quite a horrific thing to realize they were encountering a body, and probably had in their midst a murder," said Bird.

On the walls of the room where White's body was found there were satanic markings, there was photography equipment throughout the room, and there was a pile of pornographic videos on a table as well. White was positioned on a bed; her body was arranged as if she were taking part in a twisted macabre photo shoot. White had suffered head and neck injuries and there was a bite mark on her leg.

In 1888, Jack the Ripper had created a similar scene with one of his murder victims laid out on a bed. Hardy was once again emulating his hero.

Smith believed this was how Hardy now reached sexual satisfaction.

"Anthony Hardy was unable to get sexual satisfaction from ordinary sex," said Smith. "He himself had complained that it was making him very frustrated and very, very angry. It was something that he couldn't control. The sadism started to go up. The act of killing women actually provided him with some satisfaction sexually."

Hardy told police he had no idea this woman was in his apartment, let alone dead. But, there was a bucket of soapy water in the room, and it was still warm. Police wondered if Hardy had just been using the water to wash away a bloody mess.

As police began to piece together this horrific crime, it looked as if Hardy was finally caught. He was taken down to the station for a complete investigation and police believed he would be put behind bars for life. What happened next, nobody expected. A home office pathologist, who was later fired for incompetence, was sent to examine the body, he ruled the woman had died from natural causes. Hardy was once again off the hook.

"The police must have been infuriated when a coroner rules someone who is found naked with a smack to the back of her head," said Bird. "They must have been absolutely astonished that a coroner would say this was natural causes. I mean to them, they must have been convinced this girl died from a heart attack through fear."

"Had Sally been completely healthy from birth, and not had these difficulties, then it might have been that the decision that she had died from natural causes wouldn't have been so easy to come to," said Sutton.

Once it was ruled White had died from natural causes, and not murder, the rest of the evidence ceased to matter, the position she was found in, the photographic equipment, even the fact that she was found in a man's apartment she hardly knew didn't matter anymore. The investigation was finished. Hardy had once again beaten the police. Further supporting his belief, he was to live out the same fate as Jack the Ripper.

When Hardy was released from jail, he returned to his apartment and talked to Young as if nothing had happened.

"I didn't say nothing, funnily enough, he said it, 'oh I suppose you saw me in the paper.' I said, 'Tony, yeah I did.' He said, 'do you believe I didn't do it?' I said, 'Tony if you say so. Who am I to call you a liar?' And that was it. And that was all Tony said," Young said.

Although he had escaped the charge of murder, Hardy was still charged with the crime of defacing his neighbors' door. But, it was a relatively minor crime comparatively. To escape jail time, Hardy used his mental illness and convinced authorities what he really needed was treatment in a mental hospital, not a jail sentence. They agreed, and Hardy was sent for the second time in his life to a hospital instead of a jail.

"He used his mental illnesses as a smoke screen. To try and evade detection, to try and justify who he was and how he behaved," said Bird.

While in the hospital, Hardy was compliant, pleasant and good natured, once again he thought this behavior would fool the doctors and he would soon be released.

"It came to November of 2002, and there was a panel that could meet, an administrative panel, to decide on his future. And although the medical professionals would still say; 'he should stay, he should remain,' the panel came to the decision that he could be released," said Sutton.

To the outside world, it looked as if the treatment had been a success. Hardy was safe once again to enter the normal population. This time, Hardy would commit the crimes which will make him infamous, and synonymous with his long-time hero Jack the Ripper.

Hardy went back to abusing drugs, sex and pornography almost as soon as he was released. He craved more violent sex and did anything he could to get it. He wrote letters to all the prostitutes he had known in the past, trying to get them to spend another night with him.

Shortly before Christmas of 2002, Hardy meet a young prostitute named Elizabeth Valad. It was easy enough for him to convince her to come to his apartment with the promise of drugs. It would be her last day alive. Valad had fallen in with the bad crowd in high school, and after she graduated she moved into her own place, telling her family she was working as a secretary, but really working the streets. When her family found out, they tried to bring her back home, but she refused. Once she met Hardy, no one could save her from her fate.

"We know that they did indulge in extreme sex and bondage which ended with Elizabeth being strangled," said Smith. "She was then posed sexually, a devil mask, devil iconography. She was posed and photographed, which is apparently how Anthony Hardy achieved satisfaction," she added.

Weir explained Hardy's seemingly unusual fascination with taking pictures of his victims in this way; "Mr. Hardy committed a crime and took a picture of that almost as if he was proud to have committed the crime and photographed it. Some killers do respond like that. It's his work, he's proud of his work," he said.

Hardy gave the negatives of these photos to a friend for safekeeping. He had no idea he had just been given evidence of his friend's grizzly past-time.

Not long after, Hardy meets another young sex worker, Brigette MacClennan. MacClennan had a normal enough life until her marriage broke up in the early 1990's, she soon turned to drugs to ease her pain, and quickly found the only way to support her habit was to sell herself on the street. She was soon persuaded to go back to Hardy's home, where she met the same unspeakable fate as Elizabeth had just days earlier.

"Once again, the object of murder seems to have been taking these photographs," said Sutton. "There were those photographs of Bridget in similar poses to those found in relation to Elizabeth."

Smith also had an idea as to why Hardy was attacking these young women.

"He appeared to be using devil worshiping iconography, but the ritual would be more how he would achieve sexual satisfaction. That was the ritual element to this I think, and the posing of the bodies really reveals where his sexual depravities were," she said.

Two dead women were now in Hardy's apartment. Neighbors and close friends had no idea what had been going on in the building, but soon they would hear the sounds of what they assumed to be late night home improvements. Still, no one was suspicious. Hardy had planned for this event, and everything was in place. He had acquired both a hand saw and an electric power saw, and he put gloves on before he began his gruesome task. He dismembered and cut up both of the women. Once they had been cut into small enough pieces he put the remains in garbage bags and took them to a dumpster close by.

"Dismemberment is quite a horrific act. The ability to be able to do it, suggests someone who is utterly cold and calculating," said Bird.

Hardy did not seem bothered by the gruesome task he just completed, and he didn't even take care to put the remains in a trash can a greater distance from where the murders took place. The trash cans were even monitored by CCTV cameras, Hardy was well aware of this fact, and at one point, as he was walking away from the disposing of a body, he gives the camera a look, as if acknowledging its presence.

"I mean he'd already effectively got away with a crime many months earlier with the discovery of the naked body. Perhaps he was teasing people. Perhaps he was teasing the police. 'Come and get me, I'll beat you again,' " said Weir.

Hardy was convinced he was just as untouchable as Jack the Ripper was.

On New Year's Eve 2002, four weeks after the death of Valard, a homeless man was rummaging through the trash cans trying to find some scraps to eat. He felt what he thought was salmon someone had tossed out, and took it out of the can to see if anything was salvageable for him to eat. What he found when he pulled his hand out is inconceivable. It was not salmon at all, but the remains of a human leg. A leg that once belonged to one of the prostitutes Hardy had lured back to his apartment. The man called the police and an investigation was quickly begun.

Fully aware of Hardy's past, he was immediately suspected. When police arrived at his apartment, Hardy was not there, but there was plenty of evidence to connect him to these crimes.

"They found a torso wrapped in bin liners, they found a saw with flesh on there," said Weir.

Hardy had fled the scene, but as police began to discover more about his grizzly past, Hardy was finally given the moniker he wanted all along, the press dubbed him 'the Camden Ripper', after his long-time hero. Although Hardy now realized he was a wanted man, he didn't flee too far, he still needed medication to control his diabetes, and so all he did was shave off his beard and went about his business as usual.

Both Young and Reeves were shocked when they heard the news their old friend was wanted for murder.

"Never dreamed of it. No way, he didn't look like a mass murderer, or a mad ax killer or whatever you want to call him. He did not come across to me like that," said Young.

"I think I was angry, really angry that I knew somebody like that. And I can't understand, even to this day, how he could do it," Reeves added.

Hardy was soon captured, but many think even in this situation, he was still the one in control.

"I don't for one minute think Tony was caught by police. I honestly believe that Tony wanted to be caught," said Reeves.

When he was brought in for questioning, however, Hardy once again believed he would outsmart the police and get away with his crimes. Every question the police ask him was answered with a short, curt, 'no comment.'

"He wasn't trying to talk his way out. But he obviously thought that he was clever enough that he didn't have anything to say and let's see what the police can prove," said Sutton.

Much of the evidence against Hardy had been destroyed, and without Hardy's cooperation, police were having a hard time building a case.

"The hands and the heads of these bodies have never been found. The key identifying parts of the bodies. The rest of the parts of the bodies were dumped in such a haphazard fashion, almost as if he was testing the police," said Smith.

Hardy adamantly denied his involvement in either of the murders of which he was accused, but police eventually gathered enough evidence to go to trial anyway. On the day of his trial Hardy changed his mind and admitted not only to the two killings he was accused of, but a third as well, the murder of White, the woman found naked in his apartment months earlier. He was quickly given three life sentences, one for each of the three women he killed.

In 2012 a judge held up the ruling of three life sentences and also ordered no appeals could be made, Anthony Hardy was too dangerous a man to ever be allowed out of a jail cell again.

"He will never be released back into the community. He is seen as far too dangerous. And that's quite rare in fact, for a whole life tariff to be handed down," said Smith.

The mystery does not end there, though, although Hardy is behind bars, and admitted to three killings some wonder how many more he was responsible for. Several similar crimes were committed in this area of London, around the same time, and have never been solved. Is the Camden Ripper responsible for more death and dismemberment than he let on? No one knows for sure, just like no one knows the real identity of Hardy's idol and inspiration Jack the Ripper.

"The fact that he'd been able to get away effectively with all these things he was doing, or all the things we know about that he was doing, I've no doubt there was probably more to it, that he also got away with," said Sutton.

Hardy thought he was smarter than the police, and therefore would never be caught. His brazenness can be seen at several points throughout his life of violence and crime, but in the end, it wasn't smarts that saved Hardy from the police it was just lucky breaks. Once his luck ran out, it was only a matter of time before the Camden Ripper would be caught and made to pay for the crimes he had committed. Londoners can sleep just a little better now knowing this ripper is no longer out for blood.

SOUTHSIDE STRANGLER: The True Story of Timothy Spencer Wilson

NATALIE MARSHALL

Timothy Wilson Spencer has the distinction of being the first American serial killer to be convicted on the basis of DNA evidence—evidence that also exonerated a man who had been in prison after being wrongly convicted of committing one of Spencer's murders. A troubled adolescent from Arlington, Virginia, with a deep hatred of women, Spencer utilized his cat-burglar skills, strength, and agility to gain entry into his victims' homes, lay wait, and then bind, rape, torture, and murder them. In total, Spencer had been linked to five murders and at least nine rapes in both Richmond and Arlington, Virginia. He was convicted of the murders of four of his victims and sentenced to death. Spencer was ultimately executed in the electric chair on 27 April 1994.

Early Life

Timothy Wilson Spencer was born on 17 March 1962 in Arlington, Virginia, and raised in the Green Valley section of town which was known as a lower-income, tough, predominately Black neighborhood. His parents were hard workers and had attended college but had divorced when he and his younger brother Travis were young. Travis commented that their mom was the best mother ever who worked hard to support them and spent time with them.

As an adolescent he had become increasing rebellious, first getting into trouble at the age of nine and again at 12 for urinating and defecating in the school yard. He was a poor student but intelligent. In the professional literature Spencer would be classified as a life-course-persistent offender who began deviant behavior at a young age which continued throughout his life with escalating degrees of crime. He had been implicated and/or convicted of six prior burglaries (three as a juvenile) and three counts of trespassing before being arrested for burglary in 1984 for which he served three years in prison before being released to a halfway house in the Southside area that was a transitional residence for nonviolent offenders. Because Spencer's conviction was for burglary he was considered to be nonviolent even though the evidence would ultimately show that he was a deliberately violent rapist and murderer. While in the halfway house Spencer was a loner who ate at the end of the table away from others and even watched television away from the rest of the residents. He did speak to one woman who worked at the halfway house and worked on her car so that he could borrow it. Whereas among the house rules were that residents sign in and out every time they come and go and had to follow a curfew, this procedure was poorly supervised and enforced.

In an interview, Spencer's younger brother Travis reiterated his utter disbelief that his brother was capable of what he did. Burglaries and other property crimes he said he could accept but someone who displayed such anger toward and hatred of women and who wanted to control them as badly as Spencer did by the systematic torture and strangulation of his victims was too much for him to believe. He even mentioned one time in his childhood where he and a friend stole some candy from a local store and were brought home in a police car that his older brother told him to never become like him.

A big question that has remained since Spencer's execution was whether someone like him was the product of nature or nurture. Some forensic psychologists say that deviant sexual preferences are hard-wired and that when combined with certain other factors can lead to deviant and aggressive behavior. The literature suggests that predatory psychopaths suffer from atrophy of the parts of the brain responsible for moral decision-making and aggression control and whereas this may be genetically influenced, the right combination of such traits coupled with environmental influences can make someone commit heinous acts. Spencer exhibited some of the "classic" signs of the serial killer typology—bedwetting, cruelty to animals, and a propensity for setting fires—which facilitated the escalation of his actions from breaking and entering to arson to burglary to rape to murder.

The Crimes

Debbie Davis

Spencer's first reported victim was 35-year old Debbie Dudley Davis. On 18 September 1987 he entered her home through a kitchen window with a rocking chair below it and bound, raped, tortured, and murdered her. Detective Ray Williams—who was dispatched to this and each subsequent murder scene in Richmond and stated that he had never seen such disturbing crime scenes in his entire career—remarked that the intruder had to have been exceptionally strong and agile.

The assailant utilized materials found on the premises to fashion his homemade ratchet strangulation contraption and this would be a commonality at all his subsequent crime scenes. In this case, he utilized socks, shoelaces, and a 16-inch vacuum cleaner extension hose.

There was very little forensic evidence at the scene—no hair or fibers—and no witnesses which suggested that the assailant was very meticulous. Except for the semen.

Autopsy results on Davis suggested that she was murdered between 9:00 p.m. on Saturday, 18 September and 9:30 a.m. on Sunday, 19 September. At the time of her murder, Spencer lived 2.7 miles from her apartment which would be approximately a 37-minute walk. The halfway house log showed that he left at 7:30 p.m. on Friday and returned at 12:30 a.m. Saturday. Davis had spoken to her parents on the phone from 8:30 p.m. to 9:00 p.m. that Saturday evening.

She had been strangled with a sock and vacuum cleaner hose that the Virginia court said had been "fashioned into a ligature and ratchet-type device." According to the medical examiner, the contraption had been twisted two or three times, ultimately causing Davis' death. The pressure of the ligature was so strong, in fact, that her neck muscles, larynx, and voice box were cut; blood was congested within her head; one of her eyes suffered a hemorrhage; and her nose and mouth were bruised. Her hands were bound by shoelaces and were attached to the neck ligature. It was posited that the more the victim struggled, the tighter the ligature became and that the suspect did this repeated times before finally killing her.

There were copious amounts of seminal fluid at the scene on Davis' nightgown and sheets, and vaginal and anal swabs demonstrated the presence of spermatozoa. The amount of semen suggested that the perpetrator repeatedly masturbated while alternatingly tightening and releasing the pressure of the ligature on Davis' neck. Two foreign hairs were found in the victim's pubic hair that were later identified through forensic analysis as being Negroid and, subsequently, consistent with Spencer's underarm hair. With respect to the semen, investigators discovered that the suspect was a secretor, defined as someone whose blood characteristics are found in other bodily fluids such as seminal fluid.

Analysis of Spencer's blood revealed him to be a Type O, enzyme grouping PGM type 1, PGM subtype 1+, peptidase A type 1. This particular configuration is shared by 13 percent of the population; however, specific characteristics of the analyzed DNA demonstrated that the sample would match only one in 705 million Black individuals. There are only approximately ten million adult Black males in the United States.

Dr. Susan Hellams

Two weeks' after Davis' death, on 2 October Spencer struck again when he beat, raped, tortured, and killed Dr. Susan Hellams. Hellams' husband discovered his wife's beaten partially-naked body on the floor of their closet. Point of access was discovered to be a second-story window that had a large portion of screen cut from it. Detective Williams commented that this was one of the most brutal murders he had ever seen.

The medical examiner identified the cause of death as ligature strangulation from two belts around her neck. Hellams also sustained a fractured nose, blunt force injury to her lower lip, a number of bruises and scrapes, and an injury consistent with a shoe on the back of her leg. Petechiae in her eyes suggested that she had been strangled and revived for at least 20 minutes before she was killed which suggested that the assailant was likely aroused by having complete control over his victim, not unlike the Davis case. Evidence of rape and sodomy included seminal fluid on her back and in the gluteal fold; small mucosal tears of the anus; and the presence of spermatozoa on vaginal, rectal, and perianal swabs. Additionally, an ample amount of seminal fluid was found on the victim's skirt and slip. Subsequent forensic and serologic examination determined that the seminal fluid and spermatozoa were consistent with Spencer's secretion type and could not have belonged to Hellams' husband. DNA analysis ultimately proved that the fluids were Spencer's.

After Hellams' murder, the unknown perpetrator was dubbed the "Southside Strangler" and the area went into panic mode over the term "serial killer." Panic ensued in Richmond; residents of the area left their lights on all the time, every deadbolt lock was purchased from stores, and even dogs from local animal shelters were adopted in record amounts. Police had told single women to nail their windows shut. A preliminary profile suggested that he was a white adult male, approximately 35 years old, a loner, intelligent, not a criminal beginner, and likely had considerable success as a cat burglar of sorts due to his agility and ability to enter residences without making a sound.

The police sought to find a connection between the victims to help identify a suspect. Nearby Cloverfield Mall in Chesterfield County proved to be that link. Davis had worked in a bookstore and Hellams had purchased books from her.

Diane Cho

Not long after, on 22 November, 15-year old high school student Diane Cho was bound, raped, and strangled to death. Cho lived less than a mile from the Cloverfield Mall and wanted to go to medical school. She was studying in her bedroom when Spencer entered through her bedroom window and overtook her so quickly that her parents and brother who were in the next room didn't hear a thing the entire time Spencer was assaulting and murdering her.

Spencer had carved the infinity symbol on Cho which, according to experts, signified his taking, keeping, and sealing the victim for himself since she was a virgin.

Cho lived very close to the Cloverfield Mall.

Susan Tucker

While on furlough from the halfway house in Arlington visiting his family for Thanksgiving, Spencer attacked Susan Tucker, 44, in the same fashion as his other victims on or about 27 November (her body wasn't discovered until 1 December). She was home alone at the time as her husband was away on a business trip. Spencer entered through a basement window and Davis was hog-tied with a rope, raped, and subsequently died from ligature strangulation. When her body was found she had been dead for a few days and those on the scene remarked that it was extremely disturbing and unsettling.

During her autopsy four-to-eight intact non-motile sperm were collected from vaginal swabs and DNA from semen stains were determined to have been left by a secretor. As mentioned, Spencer was that secretor.

Carol Hamm

Back on 25 January 1984, 32-year-old attorney Carolyn Hamm was raped, bound, and hanged in the door between her garage and house. Her body was found naked, face down, and her robe was on the living room floor alongside a piece of cord cut from a Venetian blind and a knife.

At the time, a McDonald's janitor, David Vasquez, was arrested and convicted of Hamm's murder after two witnesses placed him on her street that day. Despite police having doubt that Vasquez was guilty because of his less-than-70 IQ, he did confess and was, subsequently, serving a 35-year prison sentence. Authorities wondered if he had a partner who might still be at large.

Absent any leads at the time, Detective Horgas visited Vasquez at the Buckingham Correctional Center near the Blue Ridge Mountains on 7 December 1988. Vasquez seemed confused; he retracted his confession insisting that he couldn't have killed Hamm because he didn't drive and had no way to get to her house after work. He also denied having an accomplice. After the interview Horgas told the warden that he believed Vasquez to be innocent.

Other Crimes

Prior to Hamm's murder, there was a string of rapes between June 1983 and January 1984 in Arlington. Nine women had been attacked by a masked Black male in his 20s who carried a knife and broke into their homes via a window and who was dubbed the "black masked rapist." The last rape, in fact, occurred on the day Hamm's body was discovered. Detective Horgas wondered whether these rapes and Hamm's murder were connected. When he heard about the first two murders in Richmond, Horgas called Detective Williams to discuss the similarities between Horgas' rapes and the Hamm murder in Arlington and the two (at that time) murders in Richmond. Williams also mentioned a recent attack in Davis' and Hellams' neighborhood wherein a Black masked man had entered a woman's apartment through a window and was in the process of tying her up when neighbors came over to investigate noises and scared him away. Whereas Horgas was virtually convinced that the crimes in both Arlington and Richmond had been committed by the same person, Williams was skeptical due to the distance between the two cities and the fact that FBI profilers asserted that serial killers are almost always White.

Williams did tell Horgas that the Richmond police were trying DNA testing which, he said, identified an individual's unique genetic material that is found in every cell of a person's body and that they had already sent samples from the Davis and Hellams murders to Lifecodes, a New York State private laboratory that analyzed DNA for paternity tests. Prior to this, nobody in the United States had ever used DNA testing in a homicide investigation.

The Investigation

All of the murders shared overwhelmingly similar characteristics which demonstrated that the deceased were the victim of a serial killer with a particular signature that was unique to him. All of the victims were bound—wrists to neck—with handmade tourniquets fashioned from materials the killer found at the house through which he could repeatedly tighten and loosen the ligatures so that he could suffocate and revive the victims multiple times. There was substantial semen left at the crime scene near the body which suggested that the suspect likely masturbated while torturing his victims. None of the victims had defensive injuries which demonstrated that they were overcome quickly. All of the victims were White or Asian with a "stocky" build. All of the murders occurred on the weekend. Additionally, in every case the victims' bodies were laid crosswise on their beds (except for Hellams who was in her closet) representing submissiveness and in each case the victims' were "covered": Davis was redressed in shorts, a sheet was placed over Cho's buttocks, a blanket was placed over Tucker's buttocks, and Hellams' closet door was closed. Some experts have suggested that posing the bodies enabled the perpetrator to extend the crime scenes to make him feel even more powerful than he already did and that his covering them was like putting a lid on a trash can. The point of entry in every case was through a window in which glass was either broken or a screen was cut.

Detective Horgas was the first to overcome what is known as "linkage blindness" in which clues exist to link particular crimes but the Richmond investigators wore blinders as to how certain cases were, in fact, linked. One of the most glaring examples of this was that Richmond police were so intent on looking for a White suspect based upon their preliminary profile and, therefore, were initially against considering the possibility that the killer was, in fact, Black.

Horgas also reinterviewed the burglary and rape victims from Arlington prior to Hamm's murder. He discovered glaring similarities and a pattern of escalation that ultimately culminated with the perpetrator "graduating" to murder. Similarities included the fact that the point of entry was always through a window; lengths of Venetian blind cords had been cut and found near the crime scenes in multiple cases; and victims had been tied up, raped, and tortured. In some cases the victims' mouths were covered with duct tape (Cho's mouth was also taped). The fifth victim was locked in a car that was lit on fire but she was able to kick her way out and escape. Perhaps most damning was that the three-year break in between Hamm's death and the other four women's deaths correlated to the time that Spencer was in prison and that for every recent murder he had signed out of the halfway house; even seeking approval for a furlough to return to Arlington for the Thanksgiving holiday.

And then there was the DNA evidence. In addition to the samples from Richmond, Horgas hand-delivered samples from the Hamm and Tucker murders as well as some of the rapes to Lifecodes on 28 December 1988.

While waiting for the results, on 29 December FBI agents Stephen Mardigan and Judson Ray from the Behavioral Science Unit at Quantico went to Arlington to examine Horgas' evidence and ultimately agreed with his theory that the crimes in both cities had been committed by the same person. The profilers said that the key to all of the crimes was to reexamine the first rape in Arlington and that the perpetrator likely lived nearby because he would have wanted to commit his first assault where he felt comfortable such as in his own neighborhood. The agents also iterated that based upon their profile, this type of person would only stop if he were incarcerated of died. This spurred Horgas to look for a suspect who was arrested and incarcerated shortly after Hamm's murder in January 1984 and released just prior to the first Richmond murder in September 1987.

Spencer demonstrated classic signatures of an anger-retaliatory rapist-murderer who utilized sexualized violence against women who are perceived to have threatened or otherwise harmed the killer's self-image. Most of these perpetrators targeted victims usually in the same age range or older than the killer; however, in the case of Cho, despite being only 15 she looked older. Since he cannot kill the actual target of his anger he finds surrogate targets who he stalks prior to the assault. Spencer punished his victims for some wrongdoing by systematically degrading, humiliating, and incapacitating them.

The next day Horgas drove to South Oxford Street where the first victim was assaulted in a nearby wooded lot after being abducted from a phone booth at South Glebe Road and Second Street in June 1983. He racked his brain trying to remember who he may have arrested nearby during that time. He and his partner Mike Hill then went through over 300 files trying to recall. Four days later the name Timmy popped into his head. Horgas remembered investigating Timmy for burglary and arson of either a house or car. On 6 January 1988 Horgas remembered Timmy's last name: Spencer. Horgas conducted a driver's license check for Timothy Spencer and found that he resided in Richmond and that he had been arrested on 29 January 1984 for a burglary in Alexandria, Virginia, just four days after police discovered Hamm's body. After serving time in prison, Spencer was released to a halfway house in the Southside area on 4 September 1987—a mere two weeks before Davis was killed. Further, Spencer's mother lived less than a mile from both murder sites in Arlington and a mere 200 yards from the Oxford Street crime scene. Horgas said that it was like a puzzle wherein all the pieces fit together perfectly. On an interesting side note, had it not been for Horgas' memory he would never have found Spencer's name in any of the parole files through which he looked so diligently as convicts released to halfway houses were not technically considered paroled.

Spencer was placed under surveillance by the Richmond Police Department; however, after a week without him doing anything suspicious the surveillance was called off. This was much to the dismay of Arlington prosecutor Helen Fahey who—not unlike Tucker—was a single woman who lived alone in a rented townhouse far too similar to Tucker's home. She contacted Horgas and the two brainstormed ideas of how to get Spencer off the street before he struck again. Fahey suggested asking for a grand jury indictment which was considerably more difficult to challenge in court that an arrest warrant.

Arrest

On 20 January 1988 at 5:50 p.m. with his grand jury indictment in hand Horgas arrested Spencer at his Richmond halfway house on suspicion of burglary.

During the drive back to Arlington, Spencer was very tight-lipped, not volunteering any statements. Horgas knew that he needed either a confession or Spencer's consent to volunteer a blood sample. Horgas asked Spencer to submit to a blood test under the guise that it was necessary to compare to some blood found on a broken window in a burglary. Unaware of the advent of DNA analysis and that a blood test could be utilized to match a semen sample, Spencer agreed, to the delight and astonishment of Horgas.

On 16 March Horgas was notified that Spencer's DNA matched fluids left at the murders of Davis, Hellams, and Tucker, as well as one of the Arlington rapes four years earlier. Both Horgas and Fahey knew they had just caught a serial killer but Fahey had to convince a jury of Spencer's guilt based upon fledgling scientific evidence that she needed jurors to understand and accept in order to obtain a capital murder conviction. In fact, due to the relative infancy and lack of knowledge about DNA evidence, trial judge Benjamin Kendrick held a special hearing to determine whether the evidence was even legally admissible. After considerable inquiry Kendrick decided that the evidence was credible and would be admitted into trial.

Trials

On 11 July 1988 Spencer went on trial in Arlington for the murder of Susan Tucker. On 16 July after only six hours of jury deliberation, Spencer was found guilty of capital murder and sentenced to death. This was the first case in the United States in which a defendant was found guilty of capital murder and received the death penalty based upon DNA evidence; a noteworthy distinction, indeed.

Spencer's Richmond trials began in the Circuit Court of the City of Richmond, Manchester Courthouse on 17 January 1989 and ultimately, on 22 September 1989, he was found guilty of rape, burglary, sodomy, and capital murder and was unanimously sentenced to death following several unsuccessful appeals of his conviction and death sentence at both state and federal levels. It didn't help his case any that when the jury was shown crime scene photos Spencer was very eager to look at them as well; essentially wanting to revisit the excitement he experienced when he brutalized the victims. Aside from this display of enthusiasm Spencer demonstrated absolutely no remorse or other emotion.

In his first appeal with Supreme Court of Virginia, Spencer raised five issues: that the DNA evidence was unreliable; that his defense team was denied the opportunity to adequately defend against said evidence because the trial court denied a discovery request for Lifecodes' notes and memoranda, that the trial court refused to provide funds for an expert DNA witness for the defense, and that the prosecution failed to reveal any evidence of problems with Lifecodes' testing process; that the trial court wrongly admitted the DNA evidence; that the prosecution improperly removed a juror for alleged racially-motivated reasons in violation of *Batson v. Kentucky*, 476 U.S. 79 (1986); and that the attached aggravating factor of "future dangerousness" is unconstitutionally vague. The Court upheld the lower court's ruling. The United States Supreme Court denied certiorari.

On 10 September 1990 Spencer filed a petition for a writ of habeas corpus with the state trial court which was ultimately dismissed on 15 November that same year and subsequently affirmed by the Supreme Court of Virginia. Next, Spencer filed another habeas corpus petition in the United States District Court for the Eastern District of Virginia which was also denied. He then requested a Certificate of Probable Cause to appeal which was also denied by the United States Court of Appeals, Fourth Circuit. An additional Notice of Appeal and request for Certificates of Probable Cause were filed in district court on 29 April 1993 and 25 May 1993 which were met with the respondent's motion to dismiss. The Fourth Circuit Appellate Court granted Spencer's application for Probable Cause.

In this appeal Spencer's legal team raised seven issues: ineffective assistance of counsel at the original trial because they failed to obtain a defense DNA expert; that he is "actually innocent" of the crimes for which he received the death penalty and would not have been convicted had he been able to challenge the DNA evidence and if the "prejudicial injection of astronomical probability ratios" had not been introduced at trial; that his trial counsel were ineffective due to their failure to conduct voir dire on the subject of racial prejudice; that Virginia's proportionality review is unconstitutional and does not allow "rational exceptions"; that the jury instructions regarding mitigating evidence were constitutionally inadequate; that his trial counsel were ineffective due to their failure to present certain mitigating evidence; and that the DNA analysis was unreliable, should not have been admitted, and, thus, his trial counsel were ineffective with respect to this evidence.

The Fourth Circuit considered some of Spencer's issues. First, with respect to ineffective assistance of counsel, the court turned to *Strickland v. Washington*, 466 U.S. 668 (1984), in which the United States Supreme Court stated that in order to prevail on an ineffective assistance of counsel claim the petitioner must demonstrate that not only did counsel perform deficiently but that the petitioner suffered prejudice as a result. Both factors must be present and the burden of proof rests with the petitioner to prove whether there was a reasonable probability that if it were not for counsel's alleged errors the result of the trial would have been different and whether there was a reasonable probability that the sentence would have concluded that other mitigating evidence would not warrant death.

Spencer's claim of ineffective assistance of counsel because of their failure to provide a defense DNA expert was dismissed due to evidence that the court not only discussed with Spencer's counsel about procuring an expert but that because no experts interviewed were willing to testify on the defense's behalf does not make his counsel ineffective. Further, his attorneys had a blind DNA test run by an independent laboratory which corroborated the evidence against Spencer.

As to the voir dire allegation of racial bias, because of the publicity surrounding Spencer's first trial in Richmond, a change of venire—wherein a jury is selected and brought in from another county due to the fear that pretrial publicity would prevent the empaneling of an impartial jury—was granted and the jury was from Norfolk. The Court held that the change of venire eliminated race as an issue with which to be concerned and that it had no reason to believe that any prospective juror had any racial bias against Spencer and this allegation was also dismissed.

With respect to the mitigating evidence concerns, Spencer contended that had his counsel adequately investigated his background that they would have discovered that his school history, presentence report, and Department of Corrections reports all stated that he was troubled; that he was emotionally damaged by being erroneously told that his father was dead when, in fact, he was not; that he regularly ingested PCP; and that he may have some degree of organic brain damage and that his counsel failed to appoint a psychologist to evaluate his mental state. The Court said that the record reflected that Spencer's counsel did, in fact, conduct a thorough background investigation which yielded evidence that Spencer's attorneys in the Arlington trial had hired both a psychiatrist and psychologist who mutually found a complete lack of any mitigating circumstances and ceased any more investigation because of fear that more incriminating evidence might have been uncovered. In fact, per the recommendation of the Richmond criminal defense bar, Dr. Robert Mullaney conducted a pretrial evaluation of Spencer and Spencer's attorneys decided to not utilize Dr. Mullaney as a witness because the sole "plus"—Mullaney's opinion that Spencer's future dangerousness would be minimized if kept in prison—was far outweighed by the potential negatives which would ensue had Dr. Mullaney testified: these being the jury finding out that Spencer committed the offense, denied his guilt, and had shown no remorse whatsoever. Further, the defense counsel stated that if they had used Dr. Mullaney then the prosecution would have been entitled to have Spencer evaluated by its own expert.

As for Spencer's claim of defense counsel's deficiency in handling adequately DNA evidence, the Court argued that his counsel did, in fact, conduct a thorough investigation and contacted several experts, some of whom assisted throughout the trial but were unwilling to testify and, therefore, determined that counsel was not ineffective simply because they could not find an expert willing to testify. Further, regarding his "actual innocence" claim and that he would not have been convicted if the "prejudicial injection of astronomical probability ratios" into the trial record had not occurred, because a claim of "actual innocence" is not a constitutional claim then—and differs from a claim of "factual innocence"— the Court's discretion was limited. Ultimately, the Court held that Spencer failed to demonstrate any constitutional error that could have affected the jury's verdict. Further, the trial judge heard all of the information regarding DNA analysis including its statistics and limitations and still decided to admit the evidence into court.

Spencer's execution date was set for 26 August 1993.

Execution

Desperate last-minute appeals for a stay of execution were denied by the United States Supreme Court and Timothy Wilson Spencer was executed on 27 April 1994. He was pronounced dead at 11:13 p.m. He was 32 at the time of his death.

Virginia author and veteran detective Lee Lofland attended Spencer's execution and described, on his website, the atmosphere at the prison as "nothing short of surreal." He stated that Spencer entered on his own, calmly took a seat in the chair, and permitted the "death squad" to secure him and attach electrodes. His face was completely devoid of any sign of fear, regret, or sadness. When asked whether Spencer had any final words it appeared that he might say something but then stopped, silently. Lofland described how Spencer made eye contact with him and even made a two-thumbs-up gesture until the leather mask was placed over his head and he was executed.

On execution day, Davis' friend Lorna Wyckoff called Spencer a "monster" and the "personification of evil." Spencer's brother Travis said it was the most difficult day of his life, hugging his brother for the last time.

Post-Execution

Whereas DNA evidence proved critical for finding Spencer guilty, it was far more difficult procuring David Vasquez's exoneration since the samples from the Hamm murder were too degraded. Vasquez would need a pardon from the governor. Fahey formerly requested the assistance of FBI Special Agent John Douglas who had founded the Behavioral Science Unit in the early 1980s after interviewing some of the most notorious serial killers in history such as Ted Bundy, Charles Manson, and David Berkowitz, and identifying patterns in their behavior; their unique "signatures." Douglas' agreement to assist was the first time FBI profilers had ever been asked to prove a suspect's innocence.

Douglas said that one must look for a signature to link similar cases and that a signature was a type of ritual performed by a suspect that is truly unique. Douglas believed that the nature of how Spencer bound his victims constituted a distinctive signature in the five homicides and that use of ligatures and ropes exceeded the necessary amount of force necessary to control the victims was also part of his signature. On 4 January 1989 Vasquez was pardoned and became the first person exonerated, albeit indirectly, by DNA evidence.

Spencer's conviction was such a landmark case because it broadened the public and professional knowledge about DNA and that the jury understood its significance and was able to convict a serial killer of capital murder was a major revelation. The case also prompted Virginia to open the first state DNA laboratory in the United States in 1989 and to set up the first DNA database.

Shortly thereafter, in 1992, the Innocence Project came into being. A nonprofit founded by New York's Benjamin Cardozo School of Law, the Innocence Project has worked to free 179 of the 337 people exonerated by DNA evidence, including 20 who were on death row. The most common reason cited for wrongful convictions is erroneous eyewitness identification with mishandling of forensic evidence due to faulty tests and/or procedural errors the second reason. DNA is not completely infallible, however. The Innocence Project states that approximately four percent of those exonerated were originally convicted as a result of improperly conducted DNA tests which have prompted virtually all defense attorneys in criminal proceedings to request retesting on their clients' behalf.

In addition to Paul Mones' (1995) book *Stalking Justice: The Dramatic True Story of the Detective Who First Used DNA Testing to Catch a Serial Killer* that focused upon Detective Horgas' efforts to link his cases in Arlington to those in Richmond and, ultimately, to

Spencer, Spencer's case provided the basis for Patricia Cornwell's first crime novel *Postmortem* (1990) as she, at the time was employed as a computer analyst in the Richmond, Virginia's Office of the Chief Medical Examiner. Former FBI profiler John Douglas devoted chapter 11 of his 1996 memoir *Journey into Darkness* to Spencer. His case also inspired the forensic science documentary *Medical Detectives* which first aired on 31 October 1996.

CANNIBAL : THE TRUE STORY OF KARL DENKE

84

NATHAN HAYES

<u>Karl Denke: A Real-Life Psychopath</u>

Karl Denke is perhaps the most twisted, disturbed man of the last 200 years. This is a man who was much more than a killer. This is a man who not only murdered over 40 people in the early 1900's, but also cannibalized them for himself and unsuspecting people. The stories of Karl Denke are beyond human comprehension; the details are simply too gruesome to understand. Karl Denke is arguably the most evil man that many have never heard of.

The life of Karl Denke is one that is largely unknown. Even his gruesome crimes and psychotic, murderous years are little known to the general public. At a time that the world was in the midst of World War I, Denke was waging his own war on unsuspecting victims in a largely contested area of Europe. Understanding his motives is simply impossible. Perhaps the worst part of the entire life of Karl Denke is the fact that he hanged himself in his jail cell before answers or justice could ever be had. Karl Denke will forever be known as one of the most twisted, disturbing human beings to ever walk the face of the Earth.

Karl Denke had a rather insignificant childhood in the fact that nothing at all special took place. Typically, cases like Karl Denke's can be traced back to traumatic experiences from childhood. That is just not the case with Denke.

Karl Denke was born in 1870 in present-day Kalinowice Gorne which is in lower Salasia. This is a largely urban area of Poland. In 1870, this was an area of vast battle for territory and political desire. Ten years later, Karl Denke was moved to Muensterberg. Muensterberg is present-day Ziebice, Poland. This is a small area of Poland known for agricultural living and urban culture. He was an extremely dull child who largely lacked personality beyond basic function. The style of living is important for his childhood in the sense that he had little opportunity to develop strong social skills.

At the age of 12, Karl Denke dropped out of school to begin working. He became an apprentice to a gardener at this time in Ziebice,

Poland. He held this job for over ten years. He had little incident and seemed to fit right in with what many young workers were at the time. He was on his way to success. At age 25, Denke's father passed away. His brother was given the family farm at this time. Karl was given a significant amount of money to purchase land in Poland to start a farm of his own. For several years, Karl tried to develop a successful farm that would lend solid profits. However, he had little experience in farming and even less desire to lead that style of life.

Karl Denke sold his farm and purchased a home in town on present-day Stawowa Street in Ziebice, Poland. Hard economic times would soon hit the entire region. A recession that rocked all of Europe would leave Karl Denke extremely vulnerable to financial hardship. Like so many other people in this era, Karl was forced to sell this property and move into a small apartment in the same town. The apartment was a one-bedroom on the first floor that famously had a small shed in the backyard. Karl Denke had hit rock bottom, but he had made it through.

In the later years of his life, Karl Denke operated a room and board home in his hometown. He affectionately did this from 1918 to 1924. He was extremely well liked by his tenants. He was commonly called "papa" by those who had been around him at this location for an extended time. For the community as a whole, Karl was very well liked and came off as very mild mannered. Ironically enough, he was even the organ player for the local church. The activities he was taking part in during this time were completely unknown to everyone around him. To everyone, he was the polite older gentlemen that they had the privilege of being around each Sunday at church. He was a great landlord who took care of his tenants in a variety of ways. The truth behind Karl Denke was completely unimaginable to everyone who around him.

The Event that Changed Everything

On December 21, 1924, Karl Denke would meet his death. The events of this day are tragic on many levels. These events also open the book on the secret life of Karl Denke. This is the day that the story of Karl Denke is all uncovered.

It was around 1 P.M. on December 21st that a man barged into the local police station in Ziebice, Poland. The man was covered in blood. It was apparent that he had been in a struggle for his life. He was shaken and stumbling on his words. He seemed to be holding on to a deep fear of whatever had happened to him. This man's name was Vincenz Oliver.

Oliver was a local vagabond. He had frequent yet minor run-ins with the law. Being as the town's population was just under 9,000, seemingly everyone knew each other. Police immediately suspected that Oliver had simply had a typical run in with the wrong crowd. What Vincenz Oliver would tell police would quickly grab their attention, however.

Oliver claimed that Karl Denke had tried to kill him with a pickaxe. Upon examination of his wounds, this seemed to match exactly with the lacerations on his body. A doctor was called in to examine his wounds further. It was confirmed by this doctor that his wounds were likely blunt force trauma lacerations. He also concluded that a pickaxe was a suitable weapon to make the kind of wounds that were present on Oliver's body. Police were utterly shocked that Oliver had named Karl Denke as the suspect. Karl Denke had a great reputation in the community. Even though they presumed that Karl Denke was likely innocent of any wrongdoing, they sought him out to question him on the accident.

Karl Denke was arrested in the late afternoon on December 21, 1924. Denke immediately confirmed that he had attacked Vincenz Oliver with a pickaxe. He explained to police that he was simply defending his property against a burglar. Police initially thought the alibi was valid. While it seemed suspicious that Denke would keep pursuing such an attack after the burglar tried to flee, they still felt like it was a reasonable explanation for the attack. Police decided to hold Karl Denke in custody while an investigation ensued.

The investigation would never see trial, however. Karl Denke hanged himself in his jail cell merely two hours after he was put in. He used his customary handkerchief to do the deed. He was found tied to the cell door by his neck. He died of asphyxiation as a result of hanging. Karl Denke has ended his own life less than 12 hours after committing a random crime against a local small time crook. His own inflicted death happened just two hours after being put into his cell. It was clear to investigators that Karl Denke was hiding something. It was their job, now, to determine what exactly that was.

A Gruesome Discovery

On December 24, 1924, police obtained a warrant to search Karl Denke's home. What the team would find is simply disgusting. In one of the most famous investigative reports in recent history, Friedrich Pietrusky documented the findings in the home of Karl Denke. Below is the official investigative report of the scene.

"The first findings made in Denke's house during the search were bones and pieces of meat. The latter were in a salt solution found in a wooden drum. There were altogether 15 pieces of meat with the skin. Two parts of the breast, which is strongly hairy. The torso is cut through the middle, three fingers above the navel. Its lateral limit is the front shoulder blade. In the piece of the anterior abdominal wall, the middle of the navel is visible. The remaining pieces belong to the side and back parts. The largest is about 40 by 20 centimeters large. Particularly striking was a very clean anus with hand large parts of both buttocks."

"The meat is brownish red and does not feel as if the body would have lost much blood. On the back some soft-bluish discoloration is visible as well as livor mortis, which leads to the conclusion that the disassembly of the body took place several hours after death."

"There is no evidence of vital reaction of the bodies to the cuts made, which means that the latter were not made while the victims were still alive. Nevertheless, some skin and muscles from the necks were missing, as well as extremities (arms and legs), head, and sexual organs. Lesions could not be determined, nor the nature of death of the tool or weapon of the crime."

"In three medium-sized pots filled with cream sauce, some cooked meat, partially covered with skin and human hair was found. The meat was pink and very soft. All pieces seemed cut off from the gluteal area. (Buttocks) One pot had only half of a portion. Denke must have eaten the other piece shortly before being arrested."

This account is a famous writing from the crime scene that details only a small portion of the findings. Each of these statement is pure fact. The last sentence regarding Denke is pure assumption however, based off of the findings at the scene. The portion was visibly gone, however it was impossible to prove or disprove that it was Karl Denke who had eaten it.

Karl Denke clearly had many skeletons in his closet, most literally. It was clear to investigators that he had killed all of these victims and dismembered them after the fact. It was also clear that much of the meat was gone. It is widely believed that Denke sold the meat at local gatherings. It is speculated that he even gave the human meat to guests that he would have over in his home. This is pure speculation however.

Pietrusky also points out some of the obvious problems with establishing what specifically happened to the meat.

"I should like to mention here that there is no evidence that Denke has ever sold the meat of his victims. All of the evidence, however, has been eaten. However, it seems certain that his guest, the vagabonds, were offered to eat it."

Could this have been the motive behind the attack on Vincenz Oliver? It most definitely appears to be the reason. Oliver knew Denke well. Vincenz knew Karl Denke well enough to voluntarily enter his home. He obviously trusted Karl and didn't know the truth behind what was going on.

Pietrusky goes on to document further. Again, each revelation that is written by Pietrusky seems to escalate in severity. The disgusting nature of the home of Karl Denke is mind-blowing.

"In the third pot, numerous pieces of human skin and parts of aorta in a gelatinous mass. A bowl on his table in his room was filled with amber colored fat, of which appeared to be human. Biological test gave a positive result for human protein."

"In the shed, in which the meat pieces were found, was also a barrel full of bones that were cleaned of tendons, muscles, etc. that most probably have been cooked prior. The investigation initially revealed the existence of six forearm bones, which means that they belonged to three people at least. More traces were found behind the shed. A part of a leg remained in the pond that Denke had dug many years before and also skeletal pieces were uncovered in the local forest. Here is a full list of what has been sent to us for examination from the forest:

-Sixteen femurs of which one pair of remarkably strong ones, two pairs of very thin ones, six pairs and two left femurs.

-Fifteen medium-sized pieces of long bones.

-Four pairs of elbow bones.

-Seven heads of radii.

-Nine lower parts of radii.

-Eight lower parts of elbow.

-A pair of upper shinbone.

-A pair of lower elbows and radii, of which extremities still remained connected.

-A pair of upper arms as well as upper arm heads.

-A pair of collar bones.

-Two shoulder blades.

-Eight heels and ankle bones.

-One hundred and twenty toes and phalanx.

-Sixty-five feet and metacarpal bones.

-Five first ribs and one hundred-fifty pieces of ribs.

"All of the bones, with the exception of only a very few, were fatless, very light, and very porous. In the forest also remained parts of a spine and clean parts of a male dissected pelvis. The pelvis showed extreme evidence of saw-cutting. Only one piece of head bone was found. This was a piece of the inferior petrosal sinus area, very jagged on the front side. It looks broken and bears considerable signs of sharp sawing on its top. This piece of bone had been cross marked with a dark ink."

"Given the size and the condition of the bones, we can assume, that there was one very strong individual and two others were of delicate bone structure."

"The cutting surfaces of the bones are very jagged, as if blunt force was applied, such as the blunt end of an axe or a hammer. Some of the bones were visibly sawed. Few spots show traces of a sharp, well maintained tool. This is most likely axe strikes. Similarly, such traces were found on the articulations, which must have been cut out with a knife."

"Based on the findings that we uncovered and upon deep examination of all of the evidence, we were able to come to the conclusion that the forest held the remains of at least eight individuals."

To put this all in perspective, the human bone collection were the initial uncovering of just the forest near the home. This doesn't take in to account the bodies of the individuals in the home or the shed. This was also just the initial findings. In the years after the initial investigation, many more bones would be discovered. In fact, the last discovery of bones from the Karl Denke case were made in the late 1940's, just after the end of WWII. The overall scope of this case is mind-blowing. Even more disturbing still was the further explanation of the investigation lead by Pietrusky.

"Considerably more revealing was Denke's dental collection. We received a total of 351 teeth from both the forest and the home of Karl Denke."

"These were found in a moneybag and in two tin boxes, on which "pepper" and "salt" was written, as well as in three paper bags, which were destined to keep pepper. They were partly sorted according to their size: the molars were in the moneybag, while the others were in the two boxes and in the paper bag. In yet another paper bag were teeth that most likely belonged to a single person, and in a third bag three lower incisors were found with strongly atrophic structure. This one likely came from an old individual. All of the teeth, with the exception of only six, were very well preserved."

The overall results the Pietrusky's team were able to conclude are staggering. He goes on to account a "final tally" of the evidence and the conclusions based off of these findings. Interestingly enough, the numbers of the victims are unknown; they can only be put to a bare minimum due to incompleteness of so many bodies. Likely, the sheer number of victims will never officially be known. It is widely agreed by several other investigations since the Pietrusky investigation that the number is much higher than has been concluded.

"The investigation led us to many important details. The remains of the bones were most definitely a minimum of eight victims, however other circumstances of the case make it likely that the overall number of victims is much higher. The teeth that were found belonged most certainly to at least twenty people. Professor Euler noted that some individual teeth appear more than twice as often as is statistically expected. This suggests that the number of victims could be even higher than expected."

"The fact that the majority of the victims suffered from caries leads us to think that the number of victims was higher. In addition, it must be stated that people in old age lacked proper dental treatment.

Professor Euler estimates cautiously that the teeth belonged to at least twenty-five different individuals."

"The extractions were done in many different ways. Some teeth seem to have been taken out quite easily due to senile atrophy, while others were rather solidly rooted and extracted with force. In several cases we discerned parts of the alveolar wand. Some specimens, especially the molars and premolars show fractures in tooth enamel that couldn't have occurred during the victim's lifetime. On some, there are traces of claws with very sharp edges. The appearance of some roots seems to justify the assumption that the jaw had been cooked in advance of the extraction. Again, Denke had no luck."

Further details of the investigation are especially odd. Typically, crimes of a similar magnitude have some sort of trend or significance to the killer. It may be the sex of the victim or the age in some instances. The investigation, using the best methods available at the time, yielded no true trend to the victims. This is not at all common to mass murder cases.

"Especially interesting is the answer to the question of the age of the victims. From the list later mentioned we know nearly all of the victims. There are no young victims among them. Now, there are four wisdom teeth that clearly came from the same individual that have peculiarities usually found on the teeth of the fifty year old. The investigation of the other teeth showed that at least four-fifths of the victims were seniors. Professor Euler summarized that among the victims there was certainly one person who was not any older than sixteen years old. The majority, however, were significantly older than fifty years old. Two individuals were probably between twenty and thirty years old and another that was likely between thirty and forty years old."

"The tests did not give satisfactory results concerning the sex of the individuals, nor their jobs. For obvious reasons, nothing specific can be said about the time that elapsed after their death. What is certain is only that some teeth had been extracted many years ago. The pulling of the tooth of a young person must have taken place weeks ago. In any case, the study of the teeth brought much more information regarding the number and age of the victims than could be learned by just the bones, but it must be taken into consideration that the latter were only partially recovered."

The next part of the account of the investigation is equally chilling. The investigation team delved into greater depths into the personal belongings of Karl Denke. The discoveries made show that Denke kept maintained records of his victims, and possibly the date of which he killed them.

"Among Denke's suspenders were three pair of human skin suspenders. They were roughly six centimeters wide and seventy or so centimeters long. The leather is not at all smooth and at one spot was broken. It seems as to not be tanned, but only free of sub-skin tissue and dried. At one spot it is quite obvious that he made cuts just under the nipples, which are still clearly visible. Four are patched with human skin taken from the pubic area. There are some traces of louse nits that were discerned under a microscope. All suspenders show traces of use and one of them was found on Denke himself."

"Besides the suspenders, Denke also had leather straps cut out of human skin, that he treated with shoe polish and parts of which were sewn together with pieces of cloth. Many of these laces were made with human hair; one sample was just one centimeter long, grey-white and, according to the study, taken from the human head."

"Equally strange was Denke's collection of coins. This consists of round, flat unfired clay pieces, size ranging from a Pfennig to fifty Pfennigs, which have just one side of the image of the coin."

"A large number of ID cards and personal papers of several different people were found in Denke's room as well as account books on revenue from the garden, on working hours and so on. They were relatively well managed and clear. More attention was attached to some loose sheets of paper on which names of thirty men and women appear. In front of every name is a date, probably the date of death of the person. At number 31 is only a date. The record is perfectly chronological. Numbering starts at number eleven. In case of women, only the first name is indicated. The notes for men are much more detailed and thorough, usually with a date of birth, place of stay, and the status of the person concerned. The assumption that this is the list of victims justified by the fact that, ID cards found in Denke's room, belonged to people whose whereabouts could not otherwise be identified. By the appearance of the sheets, we can assume, that the list had not been made in one day."

"On one side of the sheets are the initials of the name followed by a number, which most likely indicated the weight of the person concerned. On another slip of paper, next to a name stands what follows: 'dead, 122, naked, 107, disemboweled, 83'. This last figure is then repeated next to the name of the person concerned in the last table."

"Of the tools used for the killings and fragmentation of the bodies, these can be said:
-Three axes.
-A large wood saw.
-A tree saw
-A pickaxe
-Three knives.

"All of these have been seized by us with the exception of the axes and the tree saw, which are sent to be tested for traces of human blood and tissue. The saw is a large tool, with which, as the microscopic examination revealed, also had wood particles on it. The detection of human blood succeeded. However, we suppose that he used much finer tools, probably the tree saw, to cut heads and pelvic bones. The pickaxe was used for the last assassination attempt and human blood can be stated on this tool as well. It has a length of forty centimeters and is pointed forward. As for the knives, we could not make things all clear."

With this full report, it has left open one major question over all of these years: How could Karl Denke have committed such heinous crimes for over fifteen years and never been caught?

Apparently, the signs of something being off with Karl Denke were noticeable. While Vincenz Oliver escaped an assassination attempt at the hands of Denke, two other men accomplished the same thing in the decade before. For unknown reasons, however, they never came forward to police to report the crime.

The first instance was with an apprentice to Denke whom escaped the house while covered in blood. Shortly after, he disappeared and was never heard from again. Instead of reporting to police upon his escape, he hesitated, and presumably became a victim at a later time.

The second incident was a vagabond who was asked to write a letter for Denke. He soon found himself with a chain around his neck. He was much stronger than Denke and managed to escape with his life. Ironically enough, this man informed the neighbors of what had happened. This was never reported to police until after Denke's death.

The story of Karl Denke can't be summed up with just a few short words to try find a reasoning behind his behavior. Crimes such as the Denke Murder's just don't happen. The true number of victims at the hands of Karl Denke will most certainly never be known. The true scope of violence that this man portrayed can't be exaggerated. Karl Denke was one of the most twisted human beings to walk the Earth.

www.ingramcontent.com/pod-product-compliance
Lightning Source LLC
Chambersburg PA
CBHW021114130726

47988CB00003B/1024